A CD-ROM accompanies this book.
Both items must be returned in order to be fully
discharged from your card.
Any late items are subject to fines

Meeting the Needs
of Your Most Able Pupils:

DESIGN and TECHNOLOGY

Meeting the Needs
of Your Most Able Pupils:
DESIGN and TECHNOLOGY

Louise T. Davies

 David Fulton Publishers

This edition reprinted 2008 by Routledge
2 Park square, Milton Park, Abingdon, Oxon, OX14 4RN
Simultaneously published in the USA and Canada by Routledge
270 Madison Avenue, New York, NY 10016

www.onestopeducation.co.uk

British Library Cataloguing in Publication Data
A catalogue record for this book is available from the British Library.

ISBN: 1 84312 330 4

10 9 8 7 6 5 4 3 2

Series production editor: Andrew Welsh
Typeset by Servis Filmsetting Ltd, Manchester
Printed and bound in Great Britain

Contents

Foreword

It is inconceivable that a school can claim to be taking forward the personalisation agenda seriously without having a robust approach to gifted and talented education.

(Rt Hon. Jacqui Smith MP, Minister of State, Schools and
14–19 Learners, January 2006)

Effective schools provide an appropriate education for all pupils. They focus on the needs of individuals and design their offer to take account of the needs of the main recognised groups. Gifted and talented pupils are now a recognised group within each school. For a school to be effective it must plan its provision for these pupils, identify those who will benefit and monitor the effectiveness of their offer through its impact on the learning outcomes of pupils. This formalises the position of gifted and talented education and ensures that the needs of the most able are not overlooked.

Since 2000 we have begun to see the impact of a clear focus on the needs of gifted and talented pupils in the education system. The Qualifications and Curriculum Authority (QCA) and the National Strategies have begun to focus on this group and to provide materials and training to support teachers. The Office for Standards in Education (Ofsted) takes their needs into account when assessing the performance of a school and the government has established the National Academy for Gifted and Talented Youth (NAGTY) to steer this agenda.

NAGTY's role is to drive forward improvements in gifted and talented education by developing a national, government-supported catalyst that can provide leadership and support for professionals working in this field. To achieve this, it works with students, parents, teachers, education professionals, specialist providers, universities and business. Children and young people are at the heart of the Academy's mission. NAGTY aims to ensure that all children and young people, regardless of background, have access to the formal and informal learning opportunities they need to help them convert their potential into high achievement.

Gifted education in England is very much part of the overall education system and deeply embedded in it. The English model of gifted and talented education is a description of this approach and the rationale for it. Provision is rooted in day-to-day classroom provision and enhanced by additional, more advanced opportunities offered both within school and outside of it. Giftedness is a term used to describe children or adults who have the *capacity* to achieve high levels of expertise or performance. Giftedness in childhood could be described as 'expertise in its development phase'. Therefore, the education of gifted and talented pupils should focus on expertise development. Giftedness is developmental and is developed through individuals gaining access to appropriate opportunities and support. Performance levels are directly affected by availability of appropriate opportunities and support. Direct intervention with individuals can help reverse the effect of socioeconomic disadvantage or other lack of support.

Provision for gifted children should be made in ordinary schools as part of the day-to-day educational offer. This core provision should be supplemented by access to enhanced opportunities offered both within and beyond the school. Schools should themselves be diverse and distinctive in nature and so offer specific opportunities to develop certain aptitudes and parents should be seen as co-educators with a key role in supporting learning.

This series of books is a welcome addition to the literature base. It aims to help teachers make the English model a reality. In this model every teacher needs to be a teacher of the gifted. They need to understand how to teach the gifted and talented and have both the confidence and the skills to make that a reality on a day-to-day basis. While there are generic aspects to provision for gifted and talented pupils, the majority of classroom provision is subject-based and so it is through a subject approach that most teachers will consider the needs of their most able pupils. This series of books aims to help teachers within the subject domains to become more effective teachers of the gifted and talented pupils in their class. It builds on the emerging frameworks supplied by DfES, NAGTY and the government agencies and interprets them within a subject-specific context.

Without doubt this series of books will be a considerable help to both individual teachers and to schools seeking to improve provision for their gifted and talented children and young people.

PROFESSOR DEBORAH EYRE
Director, NAGTY

Acknowledgements

I thought it would be quite a demanding task to write this book on challenging the most able in D&T. And it has been that and much more. Through such a process, I was delighted to come across so many outstanding pupils and their teachers and it was clear to see how effectively the subject and its teaching and learning approaches can stretch all abilities. I shall be looking out in the future for some more famous names!

I am indebted to many people who over the years have contributed to my thinking and have added to the development of this book, I'm sure you will recognise who you are! Particular thanks go to:

- The Royal College of Art (RCA) Schools Technology Project team and especially to David Perry for 'lifting the lid' on the most able pupils; the SEN Advisory Group members at the Design and Technology Association and to the KS3 National Strategy and QCA teams who've worked with me on 'Gifted and talented in D&T' on a number of a occasions
- the well-known designers, engineers and technologists, and our young able designers for adding their words of wisdom with quotes throughout this book: Sir Terence Conran, Bruce Duckworth, Claire Curtis-Thomas MP, Paul Turnock, Wayne Hemingway, Donna Fullman, Gerry Heather, Jenny Andrews, Ben Raffles, Ruza Ivanovic, Julie Crawford, Emily Cummins, Kristina Hogg, Charlie Hull, Dominic Johnson.

Thanks also to the following for the case studies and contributions – this book would not have been possible without those stories to bring it to life:

- Mark Hudson, Thomas Telford School (for the school policy)
- Dave Coleman and Lucy from Langley Park School (for the exceptional performance work)
- Paul Shallcross, Kent Advisory Service for the Pupil Speak level descriptions
- the Bright Ideas teams for the activities in Chapter 5
- Rowena Rees for the examples from Hassenbrook School, Essex
- Michael Farmer and Rebecca Edge at Audi Design Foundation
- David Barlex at Young Foresight
- Ian Capewell at Practical Action for the Sustainable Design Awards example
- Stephanie Valentine and Sarah Schenker at British Nutrition Foundation for the A level case studies
- Matthew Alden-Farrow (www.matts.hideout.co.uk) for the dyspraxia information sheet included on the CD
- North Somerset Council Children & Young People's Services Directorate for material on the CD.

Contributors to the series

The author

During the writing of this book **Louise T. Davies** was a part-time subject adviser for design and technology at the QCA (Qualifications and Curriculum Authority), and part of the Key Stage 3 National Strategy team for the D&T programme. She has authored over 40 D&T books and award-winning multimedia resources. She is currently deputy chief executive of the Design and Technology Association.

Series editor

Gwen Goodhew's many and varied roles within the field of gifted and talented education have included school G&T coordinator, director of Wirral Able Children Centre, Knowsley Excellence in Cities (EiC) G&T coordinator, member of the DfES G&T Advisory Group, teacher trainer and consultant. She has written and edited numerous reports and articles on the subject and co-authored *Providing for Able Children* with Linda Evans.

Other authors

Art

Kim Earle is a former secondary head of art and design and is currently an able pupils and arts consultant for St Helens. She has been a member of DfES steering groups, is an Artsmark validator, a subject editor for G&TWISE and is a practising designer jeweller and enameller.

Music

Jonathan Savage is a senior lecturer in music education at the Institute of Education, Manchester Metropolitan University. Until 2001 he was head of music at Debenham High School, an 11–16 comprehensive school in Suffolk. He is a co-author of a new resource introducing computer game sound design to the Key Stage 3 curriculum (www.sound2game.net) and managing director of UCan.tv (www.ucan.tv), a company specialising in the production of educational software and hardware. When not doing all of this, he is busy parenting four very musically talented children!

Physical Education and Sport

David Morley has taught physical education in a number of secondary schools. He is currently senior lecturer in physical education at Leeds Metropolitan University and the director of the national DfES-funded 'Development in PE' project which is part of the Gifted and Talented strand of the PE, School Sport and Club Links (PESSCL) project. He is also a member of the team responsible for developing resources for national Multi-skill Clubs and is the founder and director of the Carnegie Regional Multi-skill Camp held at Leeds Met Carnegie.

Richard Bailey is a professor of pedagogy at Roehampton University, having previously worked at Reading and Leeds Metropolitan University, and at Canterbury Christ Church University where he was director of the Centre for Physical Education Research. He is a well-known author and speaker on physical education, sport and education.

Contents of the CD

The CD accompanying this book may be used by the purchasing individual/ organisation only. It contains files which may be amended to suit particular situations, or individual learning needs, and printed out for use by the purchaser.

Chapter 1 – Our more able pupils: the national scene
National agenda for gifted and talented pupils
Useful websites
Books for G&T – ideas for secondary classrooms

Chapter 2 – Departmental policy and approach
Auditing provision
Departmental audit action plan
Checklist for a more able departmental policy
Guidance on including all learners
Learning and teaching policy
Departmental policies and guidelines
Effective learning for more able pupils
North Somerset guidelines to support G&T pupils
North Somerset policy for G&T pupils

Chapter 3 – Recognising high ability and potential
Checklists of characteristics of the most able

Chapter 4 – Giftedness and learning difficulties
Dual exceptionalities article and checklist
INSET – Case studies
INSET – Strategy cards
Dyspraxia information

Chapter 5 – Classroom provision
KS4 course improvement checklist
KS3 Strategy and the most able
Resources list for Key Stage 3 designing
Design and make assignment checklist
ACCESS FM (Year 7)
Compare and contrast (Year 8)
Make a difference (Year 9)
Get out of your box (Year 9)
New from old (Year 7)
In 10 years' time (Year 8)
Word association (Year 7)

Highlights from the CD

Useful websites

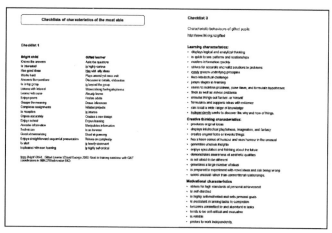

Auditing provision

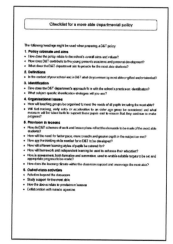

Checklist for a more able
departmental policy

Checklists of characteristics of the most able

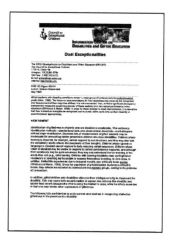

Dual exceptionalities article
and checklist

INSET – Case studies

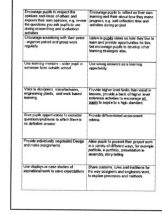

INSET – Strategy cards

KS4 course improvement
checklist

Resources list for Key Stage 3 designing

Design and make assignment checklist

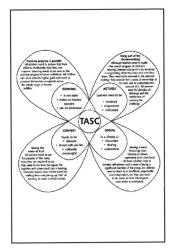

TASC diagram

The 50–50 Long shot activity

Product evaluation questions

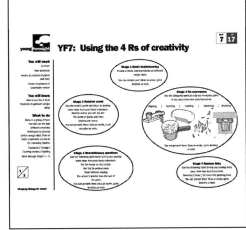

Headstart case study – Katy Linforth

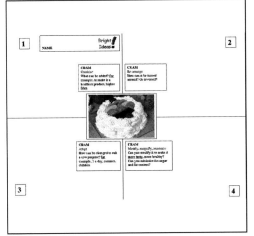

The CRAM template

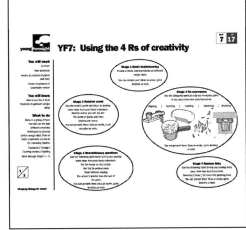

Using the 4 Rs of creativity

Introduction

If you are willing to deal effectively with the needs of able pupils you will raise the achievement of all pupils.

(Mike Tomlinson, former director of Ofsted)

Who should use this book?

This book is for all teachers of design and technology working with Key Stage 3 and Key Stage 4 pupils. It will be relevant to teachers working within the full spectrum of schools, from highly selective establishments to comprehensive and secondary modern schools as well as some special schools. Its overall objective is to provide a practical resource that heads of department, gifted and talented coordinators and classroom teachers can use to develop a coherent approach to provision for their most able pupils.

Why is it needed?

School populations differ greatly and pupils considered very able in one setting might not stand out in another. Nevertheless, whatever the general level of ability within a school, there has been a tendency to plan and provide for the middle range, to modify for those who are struggling and to leave the most able to 'get on with it'. This has meant that the most able have:

- not been sufficiently challenged and stimulated
- underachieved
- been unaware of what they might be capable of achieving
- not had high enough ambitions and aspirations
- sometimes become disaffected.

How will this book help teachers?

This book and its accompanying CD will, through its combination of practical ideas, materials for photocopying or downloading, and case studies:

- help teachers of design and technology to focus on the top 5–10% of the ability range in their particular school and to find ways of providing for these pupils, both within and beyond the classroom

- equip them with strategies and ideas to support exceptionally able pupils, i.e. those in the top 5% nationally.

Terminology

When the terms 'gifted' and 'talented' are used, the definitions provided by the Department for Education and Skills (DfES) in its Excellence in Cities programme will apply. That is:

- **gifted** pupils are the most *academically* able in a school. This ability might be general or specific to a particular subject area, such as mathematics.
- **talented** pupils are those with high ability or potential in art, music, performing arts or sport.

The two groups together should form 5–10% of any school population. There are, of course, some pupils who are both gifted and talented. Examples that come to mind are the budding physicist who plays the violin to a high standard in his spare time, or the pupil with high general academic ability who plays for the area football team.

With this definition and their interpretation of the words 'gifted' and 'talented', the DfES has created confusion and excluded achievements in D&T, because D&T is not often considered to be 'academic' nor is it included in the 'performance' subjects listed. Many teachers and designers have found this a strange omission, and have become satisfied with extending designing and making to be part of the 'arts' to make sense of an unclear definition.

'Gifted' pupils are defined as having particular academic ability in one or more subjects in the statutory school curriculum other than art, music and PE. 'Talented' pupils will have aptitude in the arts or sports, and 'all-rounders' will have a range of academic ability and talent(s).

> (DfES, www.standards.dfes.gov.uk/giftedandtalented/guidanceandtraining/
> roleofcoordinators/identificationofgt/)

Whilst we must acknowledge the difficulties civil servants have in issuing generic guidelines to schools I hope you will also recognise the sheer stupidity in this paragraph from a D&T perspective. Presumably we must conclude:

- that ability and talent are separate and different
- that ability is 'academic' – but this term is not defined other than by a list of established school 'subjects'
- that talent resides in sporting and creative activities
- that D&T is academic, and therefore not creative
- [that] therefore to achieve at a high level in D&T a pupil must be academically able but not creative.

Clearly there is a legacy here, as is so often the case, of the authors' narrow education – I would be surprised if any of them achieved in D&T at school or thereafter. Also we see here the debilitating effects of simplistic classifications.

> (David Perry, Gifted and Talented Students in D&T 2002, presentation
> at Holly Lodge School, Sandwell)

As a consequence, the more helpful terms 'more able,' 'most able' and 'exceptionally able' will generally be used in this series. Further clarification on the characteristics of most able pupils in D&T will be explored in Chapter 3.

This book is part of a series dealing with providing challenge for the most able secondary age pupils in a range of subjects. It is likely that some of the books in the series might also contain ideas that would be relevant to teachers of design and technology.

CHAPTER 1

Our more able pupils – the national scene

- Making good provision for the more able – what's in it for schools?
- National initiatives since 1997
- LEA responsibilities to more able pupils
- School Ofsted inspections and more able pupils
- Some tools to support inspection and school development plans
- Other general support for teachers and parents of more able pupils

The purpose of this first chapter is to place the design and technology content of all that follows into the more general national and school framework. We know it is easier to understand what needs to be done at departmental level if there is an appreciation of the context in which discussions are held and decisions are made.

> Today's gifted pupils are tomorrow's social, intellectual, economic and cultural leaders and their development cannot be left to chance.
>
> (Deborah Eyre, director of the National Academy
> for Gifted and Talented Youth, 2004)

The debate about whether to make special provision for the most able pupils in secondary schools ran its course during the last decade of the twentieth century. Explicit provision to meet their learning needs is now considered neither elitist nor a luxury. From an inclusion angle, these pupils must have the same chances as others to develop their potential to the full. We know from international research that focusing on the needs of the most able changes teachers' perceptions of the needs of all their pupils, and there follows a consequential rise in standards. But for teachers who are not convinced by the inclusion or school improvement arguments, there is a much more pragmatic reason for meeting the needs of able pupils. Of course, it is preferable that colleagues share a common willingness to address the needs of the most able, but if they do not, it can at least be pointed out that, quite simply, it is something that all teachers are now required to do, not an optional extra.

All schools should seek to create an atmosphere in which to excel is not only acceptable but desirable.

(Excellence in Schools – DfEE 1997)

High achievement is determined by the school's commitment to inclusion and the steps it takes to ensure that every pupil does as well as possible.

(Handbook for Inspecting Secondary Schools – Ofsted 2003)

A few years ago, efforts to raise standards in schools concentrated on getting as many pupils as possible over the Level 5 hurdle at the end of Key Stage 3 and over the five A*–C grades hurdle at GCSE. Resources were pumped into borderline pupils and the most able were not, on the whole, considered a cause for concern. The situation has changed dramatically in the last five years with schools being expected to set targets for A*s and As and to show added value by helping pupils entering the school with high SATs scores to achieve Levels 7 and beyond, if supporting data suggests that that is what is achievable. Early recognition of high potential and the setting of curricular targets are at last addressing the lack of progress demonstrated by many able pupils in Year 7 and more attention is being paid to creating a climate in which learning can flourish. Nevertheless, there is a push for even more support for the most able through the promotion of personalised learning.

The goal is that five years from now: gifted and talented students progress in line with their ability rather than their age; schools inform parents about tailored provision in an annual school profile; curricula include a gifted and talented dimension and at 14–19 there is more stretch and differentiation at the top-end, so no matter what your talent it will be engaged; and the effect of poverty on achievement is reduced, because support for high-ability students from poorer backgrounds enables them to thrive.

(Speech at the National Academy for Gifted and Talented Youth – David Miliband, Minister of State for School Standards, May 2004)

It is hoped that this book, with the others in this series, will help to accelerate these changes.

Making good provision for the most able – what's in it for schools?

What's great about design is that it's all around us. Pupils can see the principles that they're learning in school applied to real life products in everyday use. It's not like other subjects where the inspiration is difficult to find or hidden away in libraries or laboratories. I think seeing a real life application is hugely inspiring.

(Bruce Duckworth of Turner-Duckworth, who have amassed 200 international design awards. www.turnerduckworth.com)

Schools and/or subject departments often approach provision for the most able pupils with some reluctance because they imagine a lot of extra work for very little reward. In fact, the rewards of providing for these pupils are substantial:

- It can be very stimulating for D&T teachers to explore ways of developing approaches with enthusiastic and able students.

   Focusing on catch-up for borderline pupils had taken its toll. At last, I now have the opportunity to nurture those with a gift in designing and making. The rewards are many because their individual success is so high profile ... national competitions and awards. In fact, it has lifted all abilities, helped me understand practical differentiation and think about learning styles. Teaching has become a joy again.

   (D&T teacher)

- Offering opportunities to tackle work in a more challenging manner often interests pupils whose abilities have gone unnoticed because they have not been motivated by a bland educational diet.

   Some of my friends started going to the engineering and robotics after-school club and I heard about what they were doing. I like this kind of thing as a hobby and asked the teacher if I could join. Because I have not been that well behaved in D&T he was a bit reluctant at first, but then I showed him a model I had been building with my dad and he realised I was serious. The best bit was getting on TV with Robot Wars. Lessons are still not as interesting as the club, but at least I'm going to take my GCSE engineering a year early.

   (Year 10 boy)

- When pupils are engaged by the work they are doing, motivation, attainment and discipline improve.

   You don't need to be gifted to work out that the work we do is much more interesting and exciting. It's made others want to be like us.

   (Comment from a student involved in an extension programme for the most able)

- Schools that are identified as very good schools by Ofsted generally have good provision for their most able students.

   If you are willing to deal effectively with the needs of able pupils you will raise the achievement of all pupils.

   (Mike Tomlinson, former director of Ofsted)

- The same is true of individual departments in secondary schools. All those considered to be very good have spent time developing a sound working approach that meets the needs of their most able pupils.

   The department creates a positive atmosphere by its organisation, display and the way that students are valued. Learning is generally very good and often excellent throughout the school. The teachers' high expectations permeate the atmosphere and are a significant factor in raising achievement. These expectations are reflected in the curriculum which has depth and students are able and expected to experience difficult problems in all year groups.

(Mathematics department, Hamstead Hall School, Birmingham; Ofsted 2003)

National initiatives since 1997

Since 1997, when the then Department for Education and Employment (DfEE) set up its Gifted and Talented Advisory Group, many initiatives designed to raise aspirations and levels of achievement have been targeted on the most able, especially in secondary schools. Currently, a three-pronged approach is in place, with:

1. special programmes, including Excellence in Cities, Excellence Clusters and Aimhigher, for areas of the country where educational standards in secondary schools are lowest

2. resources for teachers and pupils throughout the country, such as the National Academy for Gifted and Talented Youth, gifted and talented summer schools, World Class Tests, National Curriculum Online and the G&TWISE website

3. regional support, which is currently confined to GATE A, in London.

1. Special programmes

Excellence in Cities

In an attempt to deal with the chronic underachievement of able pupils in inner city areas, Excellence in Cities (EiC) was launched in 1999. This is a very ambitious, well-funded programme with many different strands. It initially concentrated on secondary age pupils but work has been extended into the

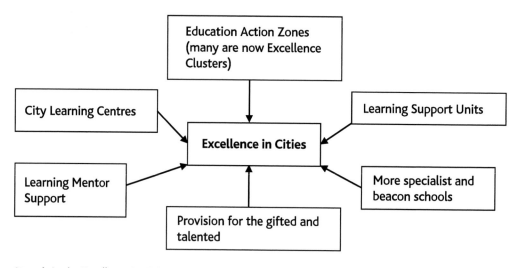

Strands in the Excellence in Cities initiative

primary sector in many areas. 'Provision for the Gifted and Talented' is one of the strands.

EiC schools are expected to:

- develop a whole-school policy for their most able pupils

- appoint a gifted and talented coordinator with sufficient time to fulfil the role

- send the coordinator on a national training programme run by Oxford Brookes University

- identify 5–10% of pupils in each year group as their gifted and talented cohort, the gifted being the academically able and the talented being those with latent or obvious ability in PE, sport, music, art or the performing arts

- provide an appropriate programme of work both within the school day and beyond

- set 'aspirational' targets both for the gifted and talented cohort and for individual pupils

- work with other schools in a 'cluster' to provide further support for these pupils

- work with other agencies, such as Aimhigher, universities, businesses and private-sector schools, to enhance provision and opportunities for these pupils.

The influence of Excellence in Cities has stretched far beyond the areas where it is in place. There are a number of reasons for this:

- Partnership (LEA) gifted and talented coordinators set up regional support groups. These groups worked to raise awareness of the needs of these pupils and their teachers. One of the most successful is the Transpennine Group, which operates from Liverpool across to Hull. Early meetings concentrated on interpreting Department for Education and Skills (DfES) directives but later the group invited universities, support organisations, publishers and successful practitioners to share ideas with them. They also began to run activities for pupils across all the EiC partnerships involved. By constantly feeding back information from the meetings to the DfES, it began to have some influence on policy. Teachers and advisers outside EiC areas have adopted similar models and the DfES is now funding regional support groups that include both EiC and non-EiC areas.

- Publishers have responded to demand from gifted and talented coordinators and are producing more materials, both books and software, that challenge the most able.

- Some LEAs have worked with Oxford Brookes University to extend their coordinator training into non-EiC areas.

- **The requirements of EiC schools have come to be regarded as a blueprint for all secondary schools.** The DfES guidance for EiC schools is available for all schools at www.standards.dfes.gov.uk/giftedandtalented.

Excellence Clusters

Although EiC was set up initially in the main urban conurbations, other hotspots of underachievement and poverty have since been identified and Excellence Clusters have been established. For example, Ellesmere Port, Crewe and Barrow-in-Furness are pockets of deprivation, with major social problems and significant underachievement, in otherwise affluent areas. Excellence Clusters have been established in these three places and measures are being taken to improve provision for the most able pupils.

Aimhigher

There have been a number of changes in EiC over the years. One of the most recent is that, in secondary schools, the EiC programme now supports the most able between the ages of 11 and 14, but from 14 to 19 their needs are met through Aimhigher, another initiative of the DfES. Its remit is to widen participation in UK higher education, particularly among students from groups that do not have a tradition of going to university, such as ethnic minorities, the disabled and those from poorer homes. Support for these pupils begins while they are still in school and includes:

- activities in schools and colleges to encourage them and raise their aspirations

- extra money to universities to enable them to provide summer schools and outreach work with pupils

- The Young People's Publicity Campaign providing information and advice to those from disadvantaged backgrounds

- financial support for students through 26,000 Opportunity Bursaries worth £2,000 each over three years for young people.

The Aimhigher website is at www.aimhigher.ac.uk.

2. Resources for teachers and pupils throughout the country

National Academy for Gifted and Talented Youth

Government initiatives for the most able pupils have not been confined to those in deprived areas. In 2002, the National Academy for Gifted and Talented Youth was established at Warwick University. Its brief is to offer support to the most able 5% of the school population and to their teachers and parents, and it is doing this in a number of ways.

The National Academy for Gifted and Talented Youth		
Student Academy	**Professional Academy**	**Expertise Centre**
• Summer schools, including link-ups with the Center for Talented Youth (CTY) in the USA • Outreach courses in a wide range of subjects at universities and other venues across the country • Online activities – currently maths, classics, ethics and philosophy	• Continuing professional development (CPD) for teachers • A PGCE+ programme for trainee teachers • Ambassador School Programme to disseminate good practice amongst schools	• Leading research in gifted and talented education

Bursaries are available for pupils from low-income families so that they are not denied access to the activities. The Academy's website is at www.nagty.ac.uk.

Gifted and talented summer schools

Each LEA is provided with money to run a number of summer schools (dependent on the size of the authority) for the most able pupils in Years 6–9. The approach to the selection and management of these schools differs from area to area. For example, some authorities organise them centrally while others allow schools to bid to run one of the summer schools. The main aim obviously is to challenge and stimulate these pupils but the DfES also hopes that:

● the summer schools will encourage teachers and advisers to adopt innovative teaching approaches

● teachers will continue to monitor these pupils over time

● where Year 6 pupils are involved, it will make secondary teachers aware of what they can achieve and raise their expectations of Year 7 pupils.

More can be found out about these summer schools at: www.standards.dfes.gov.uk/giftedandtalented/. Unfortunately, direct funding from the DfES for summer schools ceased in 2005.

World Class Tests

These have been introduced by the Qualifications and Curriculum Authority (QCA) to allow schools to judge the performance of their most able pupils against national and international standards. Tests are currently available for 9- and 13-year-olds in mathematics and problem solving. Some schools have found that the problem solving tests are effective at identifying able underachievers in maths and science. The website, at www.worldclassarena.org.uk, contains sample questions so that teachers, parents and pupils themselves can assess the tests' suitability for particular pupils or groups of pupils.

National Curriculum Online

The National Curriculum Online website, administered by QCA, provides general guidance on all aspects of the National Curriculum but also has a substantial section on general and subject-specific issues relating to gifted and talented education, including identification strategies, case studies, management and units of work. The website is at www.nc.uk.net/gt/design.

G&TWISE

The G&TWISE website has recently replaced the one called Xcalibre. It links to recommended resources for gifted and talented pupils, checked by professionally qualified subject editors, in all subjects and at all Key Stages. It is part-funded by the Gifted and Talented Education Unit of the DfES. The website is at www2. teachernet.gov.uk/gat/.

3. Regional support

At this stage, regional support is confined to GATE A, a branch of London Challenge. Four London EiC partnerships have collaborated with universities, cultural centres and professional bodies to develop a coordinated approach to supporting the most able pupils throughout the region.

Central to this is the MLE or Managed Learning Environment, which provides pupils with interactive learning materials. Some key features of this include:

- videoconferencing and online alerts for specific groups of users

- online assignments and tests

- course calendars and linked personal calendars

- personal study records.

GATE A provides five 'Student Learning Pathways' so that the approach can be matched to a student's stage of development and needs. There are subject, themed and cross-curricular skills-based pathways as well as one directed at Aimhigher students, and one for work-related learning. The initiative also strives to support the parents and carers of more able pupils. The website is at www. londongt.org.

The initiatives discussed above do not include the many D&T-specific developments, such as those from QCA, that have taken place during this period. These will be dealt with in later chapters.

LEA responsibilities to more able pupils

Schools and departments should not be shy of approaching their LEA for help when developing their more able pupil provision. Local authorities, as well as schools, are expected to support more able pupils and schools can and should turn to them for support and advice.

The notes from Ofsted on LEA Link Inspection published in December 2003 state that the main tasks of LEAs, with regard to offering support to schools for gifted and talented pupils, are:

- to provide guidance to schools in meeting pupils' needs

- to identify schools which need particular help and to ensure that this is provided effectively

- where appropriate, to support initiatives across the LEA, such as gifted and talented summer schools, Excellence in Cities, Excellence Clusters and helping pupils to access resources such as the National Academy for Gifted and Talented Youth

- to support individual pupils with particular talents in order that they make progress

- to learn lessons from Excellence in Cities areas.

After a period when many LEAs did very little to support these pupils in a systematic manner, the climate has now changed and many have taken measures such as:

- producing gifted and talented guidelines for schools

- running continuing professional development (CPD) programmes, sometimes with the help of Oxford Brookes University, which provide training for EiC gifted and talented coordinators

- encouraging federations of local schools to work together to make additional provision for the most able

- setting up masterclasses and advanced learning centres

- identifying good practice in schools and disseminating this to other schools in the authority.

Ofsted – expectations of secondary schools

The most able must be seen to have as many opportunities for development as other pupils. Poor, unchallenging teaching or an ideology that confuses equality of opportunity with levelling down must not hinder their progress. The environment for learning should be one in which it is safe to be clever or to excel.

Throughout the Ofsted *Handbook for Inspecting Secondary Schools* (2003), there are both direct and indirect references to schools' responsibilities to their most able pupils. Wherever the phrase 'all pupils should . . .' appears in this handbook, teachers need to ask themselves not only how this applies to pupils with special educational needs (SEN) and other disadvantaged groups but also how this applies to their most able pupils.

A summary of some of the more important points relating to more able pupils from this handbook is included in Appendix 1.1, where page numbers are provided so that teachers can find out more.

Some tools to support inspection and school development plans

In light of the above, teachers might find the Pre-Ofsted checklist opposite and the National Quality Standards in Gifted and Talented Education (Appendix 1.2) helpful either when preparing for Ofsted or when looking into developing this area of work as part of the school development plan. More about national quality standards in gifted and talented education can be found at www.standards.dfes. gov.uk/giftedandtalented/strategyandstrands.

It is important to remember that:

- the development of provision for the more able should be firmly enmeshed with other curricular and pastoral strategies and should fit in to the overall school philosophy

- classroom practice should match school and departmental policy.

Other general support for teachers and parents of more able pupils

Two organisations which must be included when there is any mention of support for more able pupils, their teachers and parents are NACE and NAGC.

NACE

The National Association for Able Children in Education, or NACE as it is generally known, is primarily a support organisation for teaching professionals. It has many publications on the education of more able pupils, many of them produced in association with David Fulton Publishers. Its Challenge Award has been particularly well received. Conferences are regularly held around the country and training can be provided at school, LEA or regional level. It can also provide consultancy tailored to the individual needs of schools. The Association's website is at www.nace.co.uk.

NAGC

The focus of the National Association for Gifted Children is primarily on the children themselves although it does offer support to parents and teachers as well. It can offer:

	Pre-Ofsted able pupil checklist	✓
1.	Does the school have a policy for its most able pupils?	
2.	Is there a school coordinator for the most able?	
3.	Is there someone in each department with whom the coordinator can liaise?	
4.	Are there identification strategies in place that are understood by all?	
5.	Do these strategies identify both academic ability and talent in specific areas of the curriculum?	
6.	Does the balance of the most able cohort match the school profile in terms of gender, ethnicity and social class?	
7.	Do pupils' achievements match their potential taking into account the school's performance data and other evidence?	
8.	Is negative stereotyping of the most able challenged?	
9.	Do teachers support the most able with: – high expectations?	
10.	– the employment of a wide range of teaching styles?	
11.	– a suitable pace?	
12.	– extension and enrichment activities?	
13.	– the selection of suitable resources?	
14.	Does the school's organisation of pupils into groups and sets take account of the needs of these pupils?	
15.	Does the school have an appropriate curriculum for the most able?	
16.	Do pupils have access to any of the following: learning mentors; study support; out-of-school activities; masterclasses; specialists; resources in other schools and colleges?	
17.	Are senior managers alert to the need to monitor and track the progress of the most able?	
18.	Is suitable training for staff arranged when the need arises?	
19.	Do senior managers take action when the needs of the most able are not being met?	
20.	Are the most able pupils positive about the education and support they receive in the school?	
21.	Are parents content with school provision?	

- branches throughout the country where children with similar interests or abilities can meet at regular intervals

- online activities for 3- to 10-year-olds

- counselling for young people and parents

- support through its Youth Agency for 11- to 20-year-olds with web pages to which they have exclusive access

- INSET

- publications.

The Association's website is at www.nagcbritain.org.uk.

Summary

- Schools must provide suitable challenge and appropriate support for their most able pupils.

- Appropriate provision can enhance motivation and improve behaviour.

- There are many agencies that can help teachers with this work.

- LEAs, as well as schools, have a duty to support the education of more able pupils.

- Ofsted teams expect to see suitable provision for the most able. It is an inclusion issue.

- School policy, with regard to more able children, must be reflected in practice.

- A useful summary of national initiatives, entitled *The National Agenda for G&T – an Overview*, is provided on the accompanying CD.

CHAPTER 2

Departmental policy and approach

> I have taught some very gifted children in my career and have learned that I could stifle enthusiasm for ideas very easily by expecting those students to follow my GT plan for them just because I had done one! Whereas allowing them the space to develop ideas with constructive mentoring produced blossoming ideas and super products. I soon left it to them to write their own plans for what they wanted to achieve each lesson.
>
> (Gerry Heather, SETPOINT Adviser, Bedfordshire & Luton EBP)

Meeting the needs of the most able as a department

As a part of the school and as the D&T department, teachers should endeavour to meet the needs of the most able by providing:

- opportunities for the most able to achieve to their full potential by being offered a sufficiently challenging curriculum; by being encouraged to think and learn independently and creatively

- an environment in which all kinds of achievement are valued and celebrated and in which the more able can achieve without embarrassment or fear of being stereotyped

- liaison with parents of these pupils to encourage harmonisation of home-school approaches and attitudes

- support within school to enable these pupils to cope socially and emotionally with any problems associated with their high ability. This will promote the development of self-esteem and self-confidence

- links with people and organisations outside the school to extend opportunities in specified areas.

Role of the subject leader

One of the major roles of the subject leader is in developing and managing a process for identifying pupils who show an exceptional ability in any area of study through the use of prior attainment data, screening or professional judgement. This is important as a more able pupil may have a specific ability that could go unnoticed in some areas. A variety of means will be used to identify areas or subjects in which they have very high ability.

These will include:

- information sources from outside school, i.e. parents, previous schools, specialists, e.g. educational psychologists, competitions

- information sources from within school, i.e. teacher's knowledge of pupils from observation, internal tests, pupils' written/oral work, extracurricular participation

- feedback from other adults in the school

- pupils' response to curricular and extracurricular opportunities

- pupils' self-identification

- pupils' performance in standardised tests and coursework projects.

A checklist to identify the more able pupil in D&T can be found in Chapter 3.

A full list of identified pupils will be circulated to all departments by the school G&T coordinator to allow all subject leaders to compile their own register from within the general list and from their own departmental records. The list will be organised on both a form- and year-group basis so that form tutors and year heads can effectively support and monitor the progress of those for whom they have responsibility.

The National Curriculum provides a framework for pupils to make progress at an appropriate rate, though for more able pupils there is clearly a need to develop extension and enrichment programmes based on this. It is already a requirement of the National Curriculum that schools provide a broad and balanced curriculum for all pupils. The three principles that are essential to developing a more inclusive curriculum are:

- setting suitable challenges

- responding to pupils' diverse learning needs

- overcoming potential barriers to learning and access for individuals and groups of pupils.

Thus, the subject leader will be responsible for ensuring that the department tailors its extension programmes to the needs of the pupils within D&T. Subject leaders are responsible for ensuring that these programmes are developed and implemented appropriately so that the needs of more able pupils are being met in his/her curriculum area.

In the majority of cases it is the aim to provide for the needs of more able pupils within the mainstream classroom through extension and enrichment opportunities. In some cases it may be necessary to alter an individual's timetable to allow certain subjects to be taught within a higher year group to allow for the academic stimulus and interaction at a higher level.

Teaching and learning is planned in such a way that each child is able to reach for the highest level of personal achievement. This policy ensures that the needs of those children in this school who have been identified as 'most able' are recognised and supported.

Role of the design and technology teacher

> Without the support and encouragement from my tutors, I might not have got where I am today. I think teachers are everything. My teachers were a wonderful encouragement to me.
>
> (Zandra Rhodes, fashion designer, on the value of good teachers)

Individual teachers are expected to:

- support the subject leader in collecting information about pupils' attainment

- establish high expectations of all pupils

- welcome new ideas, promote creative and imaginative responses, encourage questions and help pupils to find answers for themselves

- praise excellence just as much as any other pupil

- help the more able child understand that failure to succeed can be a positive experience

- encourage the more able child to relax and have fun at certain times.

A coordinator in the school will also support the subject leader and teachers.

Role of the school coordinator in the provision for gifted and talented or most able pupils

Provision for gifted and talented pupils is a whole school issue. Ofsted findings suggest that there are pockets of good provision in most schools – maybe particular teachers or certain subject departments. However, effective provision throughout the school is still just an aspiration for many schools. Therefore, the leadership team within a school needs to take responsibility for providing an infrastructure that delivers consistency of provision.

Schools that make effective provision for their gifted and talented pupils factor their needs into the full range of school structures including: creating a policy, considering the core curriculum offer, looking at ways to offer enhanced opportunities within and beyond the school, the pastoral support system, pupil grouping, assessment approaches, use of pupil data and tracking, identification of gifted and talented pupils, teaching and learning approaches, opportunities for fast tracking cohorts of pupils or the acceleration of individuals, working with parents, listening to pupils.

Almost all effective schools have a designated coordinator for gifted and talented pupils, who lead activity on improvement on behalf of the leadership team and acts as an expert in the school.

The coordinator will:

- set up a system for identifying high levels of ability

- provide support for teachers on the use of appropriate practice

- consult with staff at all levels and ensure that all relevant information is communicated to them

- encourage staff to participate in INSET

- communicate all relevant information to governors through the appropriate channels

- encourage good home–school relationships and liaison

- identify and develop the resources needed (materials, staffing and expertise) for the implementation of the policy

- promote the use of resources from the wider community, including suitably qualified adults.

The coordinator will also monitor and review provision on an ongoing basis by:

- keeping a register of most able pupils

- monitoring the progress made by identified pupils

- ensuring that all staff are aware of the process of identifying the most able pupils and that the process is undertaken when appropriate

- ensuring that activities for the most able are identified on short-term plans where appropriate

- reviewing the opportunities being offered in the school

- reviewing schemes of work to confirm the opportunities being offered by subject and the classroom

- scrutinising National Curriculum Assessments and moderation procedures.

Opportunities to reveal exceptional ability

In order to give every pupil an opportunity to show whether they are gifted or talented, schools should promote an open-minded approach to their identification. This can be described as a portfolio approach, where information from a wide variety of sources is gathered and examined. This information should come from a range of sources, including the pupil's teacher and parents, and should be both objective and subjective. Thus work samples and test results will be included along with observations and nominations from those within, and outside of, the school.

Ultimately a great deal of reliance will be placed on the classroom teacher's nomination. Research shows that teachers' ability to recognise giftedness is varied, which is understandable given the historically low levels of training teachers receive in catering for the gifted pupil. It is worth noting that teachers will only be able to observe many of the characteristic behaviours of the gifted pupil if they have a classroom environment where these behaviours can occur. Questioning, risk-taking, persistence, creativity, problem solving, making connections and seeing to the heart of a problem are some of the characteristics of gifted pupils in D&T. In a constrained classroom these behaviours may never have the opportunity to arise. There is a need to 'set the scene' by fostering an environment where these characteristics are accepted and valued, and by providing the following in D&T:

- **Choice:** gifted pupils will be more likely to exhibit perseverance when they have ownership of the task.

- **Degree of difficulty:** make some of the choices more difficult than you would normally and note who attempts them.

- **Open-ended:** provide tasks that are open-ended in nature so that pupils can go beyond the normal constraints of workshop tasks and really show what they are capable of.

When the task is challenging and interesting, pupils will tend to self-select themselves by their response. Look out for those pupils who

- are intensely focused

- ask insightful questions

- see beyond the obvious

- thrive on complexity

- make abstract connections

- provide creative and original solutions.

Carrying out a D&T audit of provision

Many schools will have used the D&T audit that accompanies the Key Stage 3 National Strategy. The Most Able audit included on the CD uses some of the strategies included in that document, but also includes others that relate directly to provision for the most able.

Stage 1 Collecting and analysing information

The subject leader and the departmental staff will need to collect and analyse information such as:

1. Who have we identified as the 'most able' cohort (top 5–10%)?

- Are there any groups whose performance at the top-end is under-represented in D&T? For example, pupils who receive free school meals, boys, girls, ethinic minority groups?

- What are their current levels of attainment (national curriculum levels)?

- How many pupils achieve level 5 and above, and how does this school compare with others.

- How many pupils opt for this subject at GCSE and AS/A Level?

- How do the most able pupils react to the subject – enthusiastic, noncommital, disengaged? Can you pinpoint why?

- What extracurricular support/activities are provided for the most able in each year group?

2. What do we currently do about the 'most able' in the D&T department?

- Has the department developed a policy on its provision for the more able?

- Does it have a more able/G&T coordinator or representative who liaises directly with the school more able/G&T coordinator?

- Are the most able students clearly identified in subject registers?

- Has the department identified CPD requirements in relation to more able pupils?

- Has the department agreed the strategies it will use to provide suitable pace, depth and breadth for the most able? Does the department have an agreed approach to providing for the exceptional child whose needs might not easily be met in the ordinary classroom?

- Does short-term planning outline expectations for the most able and any extended/modified tasks for them?

- Are there suitable resources for the most able?

- Is homework used to extend the most able?

- Do the most able have plenty of opportunities to develop as independent learners?

- Are different learning styles taken into account when planning for and assessing the most able?

- Do you keep a portfolio of outstanding work in your department?

- Is provision for the most able regularly discussed at departmental meetings?

- Do you share good practice in more able provision with other departments or schools?

- Is the progress of your most able students effectively monitored?

Stage 2 Following up the audit

After this audit, team discussion and planning is required to achieve effective provision. It will be important to:

1. highlight all areas where achievement or provision in your department is lacking

2. decide on about three priorities to raise standards or improve provision for your most able

3. draw up an action plan including:

   - what your success criteria are or what you hope to achieve

   - action to be taken

   - when action will be taken and by whom

   - where you will go for help

   - what resources you need

   - how you will monitor your progress

   - what your deadline is for assessing your success.

An action plan template is included on the accompanying CD.

What to include in a more able or gifted and talented D&T policy

The D&T policy should follow the same framework as the school policy and fit in with its general philosophy. A good policy will develop from:

- a thorough and honest audit of existing levels of achievement of the most able and of their attitudes to learning

- clear identification of where changes need to be made and the drawing up of an action plan

- consultation with senior management, G&T coordinator, other staff in the department and pupils

- the existence of effective strategies to monitor and evaluate the measures taken.

The following headings might be used when preparing a D&T policy. There are also six different examples from schools for you to see, as well as these headings as a simple checklist on the CD.

1. **Policy rationale and aims**

   a. How does the policy relate to the school's overall aims and values?

   b. How does D&T contribute to the young person's academic and personal development?

   c. What does the D&T department aim to provide for the most able students?

2. **Definitions**

   a. In the context of your school and in D&T what do you mean by most able or gifted and/or talented?

3. **Identification**

   a. How does the D&T departments' approach fit in with the school's practice on identification?

   b. What subject-specific identification strategies will you use?

4. **Organisational issues**

   a. How will teaching groups be organised to meet the needs of all pupils including the most able?

   b. Will fast tracking, early entry or acceleration to an older age group be considered and what measure will be taken both to support these pupils and to ensure that they continue to make progress?

5. **Provision in lessons**

   a. How do D&T schemes of work and lesson plans reflect the demands to be made of the most able students?

   b. How will the need for faster pace, more breadth and greater depth in the subject be met?

   c. How are the thinking skills needed in D&T to be developed?

d. How will different learning styles of pupils be catered for?

e. How will homework and independent learning be used to enhance their education?

f. How is assessment – both formative and summative – used to enable suitable targets to be set and appropriate progress to be made?

g. How does the learning climate within the classroom support and encourage the most able?

6. **Out-of-class activities**

   a. activities beyond the classroom

   b. study support for the most able

   c. how the above relate to provision in lessons

   d. collaboration with outside agencies.

7. **Transfer and transition**

   a. How is information from primary schools used to ensure progression?

   b. What measures are taken to assist the most able pupils during their transition from primary to secondary school?

   c. How are students, who move on to sixth forms in other schools or colleges, supported?

8. **Resources**

   a. How are teaching assistants, learning mentors and other adult helpers used to support the most able?

   b. What outside agencies are used?

   c. What specific learning resources are available for the most able?

   d. How is ICT used to enhance the education of the most able?

9. **Monitoring and evaluation**

   a. Who is responsible for liaising with the school coordinator and developing good practice for the most able in your department?

   b. How is the effectiveness of this policy to be measured?

   c. What targets does the department have for its most able students (e.g. Levels 7 and 8 at Key Stage 3, A* and A at GCSE)?

   d. How and when is the progress of individual students and groups monitored?

   e. What CPD is needed or will be provided?

Key extracts from the D&T policy at Thomas Telford School

Equal Opportunities/race/cultural

The faculty fully supports the school policy on Equal Opportunities. Staff should be aware of the traditional stereotypes that apply to elements of Design and Technology and make efforts to break these down. All pupils should have equal opportunity and access to all elements of the subject. Pupils should be made aware of gender issues in the employment areas that the subject has a major contribution to. Staff will, wherever possible, ensure that cultural issues are dealt with in line with school policy. This curriculum area offers ample opportunity to celebrate cultural diversity in the fields of design and technology. Staff should seek advice if unsure how to incorporate aspects of this policy into their teaching.

Pupil groupings

Pupils are placed into broad mixed ability bands for all areas of technology. From Module 7 students will move to specialised groups. The groupings are reviewed by faculty staff, based on performance within the subject areas and group dynamics.

New pupils will be placed in the group most appropriate at the time the pupil joins the school, based on information available. Attempts will be made to ensure equity of numbers in groups.

SEN

The DHM holds a file detailing the students with special needs. Staff should be aware of the needs of students. Staff are requested to sign to indicate that they have read the file and noted necessary strategies recommended. Staff are reminded that SEN also cover the needs of exceptionally able. These students should be noted on session planning and differentiation strategies applied accordingly. These students will also be considered for fast track in Y10 entry. In Y9 these students should be identified for inclusion in the Smallpeice trust schemes; these are residential and usually lead to subsequent offers of places on specialised courses at university. Students will normally be granted permission to absent themselves for these courses. Other opportunities exist through the Arkwright scholarship in Y11 and Engineering Education scheme.

Reviewing schemes of work and teaching approaches for the more able

Don't worry about giving advice – but try not to stifle creativity. However, be prepared to argue – creative people tend to be in a world of their own. I wanted to make a large metal chair that could hang from the ceiling; my teacher had to talk me out of it because, it just wasn't practical for an A level project.

(Charlie Hull, Audi Young Designer finalist)

Curriculum needs

Much of the education a gifted child needs is the same as for other pupils:

- carefully planned acquisition of appropriate knowledge, skills and key concepts
- clear learning objectives that are shared with the pupils
- negotiated targets
- high expectations
- variety of teaching approaches and learning styles
- an opportunity to evaluate their projects and their learning and for the teacher to get feedback on their teaching.

In addition, more able pupils need to **develop greater expertise** through access to activities in the scheme of work that encourage:

- higher order thinking (i.e. in more complex product evaluation)
- reflection (i.e. thinking about how a product may be used or even misused and social impact of the design)
- exploring a variety of views (i.e. reconciling the needs of a variety of people involved in using a product)
- considering difficult questions (i.e. working beyond their experience and formulating questions that their design will need to address)
- developing individual opinions (i.e. analyse their research, apply what they found out to their ideas and be able to justify their decisions)
- problem solving (i.e. taking on a design brief for their company during work experience and presenting some solutions)
- connecting past and present learning (i.e. having a repertoire of designing strategies that they have learned and choosing the most effective one)
- independent learning (i.e. choosing and negotiating projects of their own choice, interest).

Planning an effective D&T scheme of work that is inclusive of more able pupils requires adding **breadth, depth and pace** to the standard D&T scheme.

Social and emotional needs

> Let the child explore and experiment as much as they want to; however crazy don't try and hold them back.
> (Emily Cummins, Audi Young Designer finalist)

Being a more able child can be an isolating lonely experience! In D&T achievements are very public, and the designed and made product is constantly on view to the rest of the class. This can cause tension between the able child and his/her peers, increasing the sense of isolation. Some able children often describe themselves as 'odd' or different and end up set apart from their classmates. They make some friends, but provision is required to make sure that these pupils get to work with others at their level, their intellectual equals – to lessen this social and emotional impact. Young gifted people between the ages of 11 and 15 frequently report a range of problems as a result of their abundant gifts: perfectionism, competitiveness, unrealistic appraisal of their gifts, rejection from peers, confusion due to mixed messages about their talents, and parental and social pressures to achieve, as well as problems with unchallenging school programmes or increased expectations. Some encounter difficulties in finding and choosing friends, a course of study and, eventually, a career. The developmental issues that all adolescents encounter exist also for gifted students, yet they are further complicated by the special needs and characteristics of being gifted.

What does it mean to make progress in D&T?

> Encourage them to think outside the box and be creative, enter competitions, so that they can talk about their work and gain credit for it.
> (Kristina Hogg, Audi Young Designer finalist)

To understand how to add breadth, depth and pace it is important to know what it means to make progress in D&T.

Pupils will progressively:

- increase their knowledge and skills so that they know and understand more and are more skilful than when they started

- move from familiar to unfamiliar contexts

- meet needs that demand more complex or difficult solutions

- become able to see new goals, to see things that they can intervene in and do

- develop personal autonomy, self-directness, the ability to manage themselves and their personal resources

- increase understanding of their own learning and how they can progress.

The table opposite illustrates the progression for most pupils across Years 7–9 and was used to underpin the Key Stage 3 strategy framework for D&T.

Progression in D&T capability

One of the distinctive features of D&T is that it is not about pupils learning a particular piece of knowledge or skill, and that the concepts they learn simply become harder. The process of doing D&T requires them to integrate knowledge, understanding and skills into some sort of solution. They develop their ability to synthesise their knowledge, skills and understanding, and use them coherently

Progression in Key Stage 3

Exploring	Generating ideas	Developing/modelling ideas	Planning	Evaluating	Making
Year 7					
• Looking for needs, wants and opportunities • Designing for yourself	• Learning to think and intervene creatively • Responding to needs, wants and opportunities • Developing a range of design skills and use them to effect change • Making connections and seeing relationships	• Exploring a range of strategies to develop their thinking and capacity to effect change. • Playing with ideas, keeping options open • Using a range of communication techniques as a means of self-reflection and to describe their design ideas, thinking and planning	• Learning when working with others • Developing planning skills • Working independently on well-defined tasks • Sharing decisions with the teacher and others	• Evaluating strengths and weaknesses – how well does it work? • Evaluating products in relationship to users	• Making for yourself • Understanding materials
Year 8					
• Designing for clients • Questioning and challenging • Asking unusual questions, respond to ideas, tasks or problems in an unusual way, challenging conventional responses, independent thinking	• Developing flexible and independent thinking, encouraging questioning, openness to ideas and different ways of doing things	• Understanding and using the relationship between different design skills to become better designers • Representing ideas in different ways. Create, recreate, interpret and communicate ideas effectively in unexpected ways • Selecting appropriate communication techniques to document and convey clearly design ideas, thinking and organisation	• Negotiating tasks with the teacher and others • Adopting different roles within a group • Managing time within a lesson. • Bringing resources together at the right time • Working independently on a task determined by the teacher	• Evaluating and modifying • Explain the choices and decisions made in designed and manufactured products, processes and systems and identify alternative possibilities	• Producing batches • Exploring materials
Year 9					
• Designing for markets • Envisaging what might be	• Stimulating the imagination • Sharing work with others, gathering constructive feedback	• Integrating design skills to create personal strategies for designing culturally, environmentally and socially defensible products, processes and systems • Evaluating effects of ideas and actions • Demonstrating skills in using a broad range of recognised communication techniques to convey design thinking	• Work facilitated by the teacher or others • Working independently on a chosen task • Choosing to adopt an appropriate role within a group, such as negotiator, leader, etc • Managing own time across a number of lessons • Prioritising and reconciling decisions on materials, time and production	• Evaluating the wider impact of products • Identifying and using criteria to judge the quality of products	• Ensuring quality production • Selecting materials

to make design solutions. Thus, pupils draw on their knowledge, understanding and skills in order to design and make products.

It is important to structure what pupils learn as knowledge (the 'what') and skills (the 'how to'), but it is even more important to teach them how to draw on this knowledge when designing and making (the process), which is why the framework pays particular attention to the process of designing.

The concept of progression in D&T capability is characterised by the simultaneous development of pupils'

- propositional knowledge (knowing that)

- tacit knowledge (knowing how to)

- process skills.

'Knowing that' works together with 'knowing how to' and enhanced process skills to bring all this knowledge to bear in a purposeful constructive manner. Progression consists of pupils' ability to apply this knowledge and these skills to their designing and making and to continuously improve their quality of understanding, their purposes and the outcome.

Progression in D&T encompasses:

- the development of the ability of the pupils to handle individual concepts of increasing breadth and depth

- the ability to handle a large number of increasingly complex concepts simultaneously.

These D&T concepts include:

- **knowledge** of products, health and safety, materials, aesthetics, human needs, technological systems, resources, equipment and processes

- **values and attitudes**, such as creativity, ingenuity, care, confidence, resourcefulness, flexibility, sensitivity, decisiveness, cooperation, independence, social responsibility

- **skills**, such as investigating, analysing, identifying needs, offering and communicating ideas, exploring and appraising ideas, developing and recording ideas, working with materials and equipment, practical skills, managing resources, planning, making, evaluating, etc.

Thus **pupils make progress in their ability to handle individual concepts**, such as evaluating existing products, by looking at more sophisticated techniques for evaluating a wider range of products, and more complex issues that require careful investigation and information gathering to come to a judgement.

But also, **pupils will progress in their ability to handle a number of concepts at the same time** – for example the ability to be able to design and make a product that requires them to draw on a number of aspects at the same time, for example health and safety, materials science, resource management and social responsibility.

One important step in planning for progression for more able pupils in a scheme is to identify the dimensions along which pupils can progress. While there are a number of additional skills and concepts one might identify to add depth and breadth, it is important to remember that pupils **develop their capability in a holistic way through combining their designing and making skills with knowledge and understanding to make quality products**. Most teachers will also know that individual pupils learning year-on-year is not quite as systematic as we might hope, as each individual will have strengths and weaknesses. Teaching can be structured progressively, but individuals will make their own progress route. Learners do not necessarily advance in an orderly manner and we have all witnessed or experienced leaps in understanding when things 'fall into place' at once. Teachers need to involve pupils in planning their own progress. Pupils can be encouraged to take responsibility for their own learning and objectives can be shared with them.

Effective timetabling and rotational courses

Rotational or carousel courses are common in D&T departments. Pupils meet a new focus area and teacher every 8–10 weeks. This is hugely detrimental for more able pupils. Evidence shows that **frequently rotating pupils around different materials areas often results in a lack of progression**. Rotational courses have also been shown to be frustrating and exhausting for pupils and teachers alike. Pupils can be constantly rushed, lack time for the reflection that reinforces learning, and become disenchanted with achieving lower standards as a result. Teachers who experience a rapid turnover of large numbers of pupils, having very limited contact with any of them, are given little opportunity for the satisfaction that comes from nurturing their pupils' progress over time. They are very unlikely to have time to identify the more able pupils, let alone develop work for them that adds breadth, depth and pace!

These problems can be avoided if staff plan, as a team, to ensure that they introduce greater demands, which build on earlier experiences as pupils progress through a year.

A closely informed staff team can lessen these disadvantages for each other and ensure that together they achieve good oversight of each pupil's progress through a year and key stage.

However, **fewer, larger blocks of time**, possibly involving two teachers working collaboratively in two focus areas, lessen the disadvantages of rotational schemes, but again, only if high-quality team planning is assured.

Staff will need time to plan together and to develop a team approach. This will result in improving standards because pupils transfer their learning across materials areas and build on skills rather than repeating them and will do so within a programme that explicitly focuses on this transfer of learning. It also means that pupils do not spend short periods of time with an excessive number of different teachers.

How one team approach works in practice

In a school that follows the model supported by the Design and Technology Association (DATA) and DfEE (1997), two teachers will work in parallel and are timetabled throughout a whole year to share responsibility for one class. One teacher would be responsible for resistant materials and the other for food and textiles work, taking a common approach to designing and using complementary approaches for developing graphic and other communication skills, control systems and structures.

Two Specialist Design & Technology Staff working in parallel with one class over a year	*Links with science, art and design, and mathematics*		
	TEACHER 1 **Resistant and compliant materials, elements of control systems, structures and IT**		
	The same approach to designing through the use of a common framework for learning		
	A common and complementary approach to communication including graphics		
	TEACHER 2 **Food and/or compliant materials, elements of control systems and IT**		
10%	Year 7	Year 8	Year 9

The 1997 DATA/DfEE model for sharing teacher responsibility

Moving on from rotational courses

D&T teachers at Brune Park Community College in Hampshire were interviewed as part of QCA research into the effects of rotational courses and they described what their system used to be like and why they changed it to a non-rotational course:

> Pupils on a carousel system could be taught by ten different D&T teachers during years 7 and 8, and as a result of this no teacher would really know the pupils as individuals. Continuity of progression and assessment in a carousel system is difficult to achieve and there is no flexibility in the time of units.
>
> The new system allows for better continuity and progression for pupils and for their strengths and weaknesses to be known by the teacher, leading to greater individual support. In addition, units of work have a longer running

time, allowing enough time for the designing rather than rushing to start the making in order to get it finished in time. The year 9 structure means there is less disaffection from pupils studying a material area in year 9 that they no longer enjoy, have success in, or value. Higher-level teaching occurs in year 9 prior to GCSE, due to more highly motivated pupils. Pupils and teachers develop stronger relationships and teachers can better plan differentiation for individuals and effective progression for groups. Target-setting is improved, as there are just two teachers involved with any pupil. Time can be used more flexibly. Disaffection in year 9 is reduced and progress is faster. Year 10 pupils are better prepared and make faster progress.

CHAPTER 3

Recognising high ability and potential

> So many gifted children go through their childhood without ever being told that they are very special – so often, the pleasure of introducing a child to their own unique ability is left to the teacher – positive affirmation, praise and recognition is priceless and could liberate a young person to realise their innate capability.
>
> (Claire Curtis-Thomas MP)

Take a moment to list the most able product designers, engineers and technologists you can think of . . . Wayne Hemingway, Isambard Kingdom Brunel, Jonathan Ive, Jamie Oliver . . .

I wonder what they were like at school . . . Were they brilliant across all subjects? Were they brilliant in D&T? Were they brilliant at particular things such as handling tools, visualising, connecting ideas? Did they hide their talents or show them off? Did they question their teacher?

I wonder if their ability was recognised by the teacher at the time. What should a teacher look for?

Recognising high ability

There are a variety of ways in which pupils may show that they have high ability or potential in design and technology.

Performance in all subjects

An indicator that a pupil is very able may be that they perform generally well across all school subjects, thus tests and results for English, maths and science may provide some clues to identifying a pupil who is very able in D&T. However, in many instances, those pupils that are most able in design and technology may be a very different group of pupils than those recognised as high ability in other subjects. Many extraordinarily talented D&T students do not perform well in so-called 'academic' subjects.

Test and exam performance in D&T

> Believe in yourself even if your teachers don't. Many a good designer has poor exam results or in fact no exams . . . Gerardine Hemingway left school @ 15 !!!
>
> (Wayne Hemingway, www.hemingwaydesign.co.uk)

Another indicator may be national curriculum levels and year-end tests in D&T. Some pupils may perform at national curriculum levels that are unusually advanced for their age group, for example achieving level 8 at Year 7, or A* effortlessly. Thus we can use QCA attainment target descriptions for levels 7, 8 and exceptional performance to help us to identify pupils (see p. 33). We can also use A grade GCE/GCSE grade descriptions (see p. 36).

However, high-ability pupils in D&T do not always demonstrate outstanding achievement in tests and exams or display particular enthusiasm for the subject. Indeed, a very creative pupil is often not recognised in the current GCSE and A Level examinations where pupils are tightly directed to meet very specific coursework requirements, and rigid structures for portfolio submissions. The most able pupils can fail miserably as they find this approach constraining and frustrating, so they become demotivated. In trying to conform, they often perform far below their true capability. Their unconventional approaches or skills remain uncredited in the traditional exam.

Indeed 'All our Futures: Creativity, Culture and Education' (NACCCE 2000) pointed out that while schools have a duty to meet pupils needs – social, spiritual and emotional as well as academic – and to help youngsters make sense of their lives by discovering their own strengths, passions and sensibilities, the academic curriculum and its associated testing systems are not designed to do this.

D&T level descriptions also describe capability across the breadth of designing and making, including the wide range of materials and contexts. A pupil may have distinctive ability in one or two particular aspects, for example working with food, using CAD, high-quality craft-making where a particular skill is used. They do not score highly across D&T as a whole, but they can be seen to be most able in very specific aspects of it. If you were to use the level descriptions as a checklist, pupils may not display the breadth required to achieve Levels 7, 8 and EP. These descriptions also omit some aspects that the most able are likely to demonstrate such as risk-taking, innovation, intervening creatively, thinking divergently, and the ability to synthesise ideas and manage complex conflictions.

Exceptional ability, for various reasons, may not result in high attainment in tests and it is important to identify pupils with high-level potential in addition to those with high-level achievement.

Observing able pupils in action

It is essential to provide opportunities in the classroom that allow all pupils to demonstrate their special abilities in design and technology. The outcomes of specific tasks, evidence of particular aptitudes, the responses to questions asked by the teacher and the questions asked by the pupils themselves may all contribute to the identification of pupils who are most able.

Whilst some pupils are keen to show their ability others may be more reticent, not wishing to appear different from their peers. Some pupils go to great lengths to hide their abilities from others.

Personal interaction between teacher and pupil that enables the teacher to observe techniques and strategies used by the pupil in tackling problems is helpful in finding out things about a pupil which may not be evident through more formal assessment procedures.

What to look for

It has to be said that pupils may exhibit negative and positive characteristics. One difference that teachers remark upon between able and most able is that **able pupils** are often a pleasure to teach – well-motivated, interested, forthcoming, happy, well-adjusted, well-organised . . ., whereas the **very able** may be critical, demanding, intense, intolerant, unable to get on with peer group, untidy, disorganised, not always motivated . . . underachieving.

Some typical characteristics

The very able D&T pupil may demonstrate any, but certainly not all, of the following behaviours:

- underchallenged, low motivation, disaffected, leading to self-fulfiling underachievement

- conform quietly, take easy options and attain at an adequate level so as not to draw attention to themselves

- avoid work openly, be highly vocal and dismiss the subject as not important, 'I'm no good because I don't care'

- become irritated when a teacher demands that they follow a rigid design and make process

- flashes of inspiration, highly original or innovative ideas, different ways of working approaches to issues

- demonstrate high levels of technological understanding

- sensitive to aesthetic, social and cultural issues when designing

- rigorous analysis and interpretation of products

- high-quality making and precise practical skills

- able to work comfortably in contexts beyond their own experience and empathise with users and clients needs and wants.

Classroom assessment opportunities

It is very helpful to build in opportunities when you meet a class for the first time to allow individuals to show you how much they are capable of. For example, at the start of Year 7, too often pupils spend time being drilled in the routine of the practical room and its safety points, when valuable time could be spent getting to know the pupils' strengths and aspirations. An open rather than closed design brief for the first project can be more revealing and could be used as an assessment task. One department changed their first design brief from *Key Fob*:

> Secure IT Ltd is a company that specialises in producing security items for the home. This firm has asked you to design and make an attractive acrylic key fob that may be sold in the company's shops. The key fob would enable the customers to keep all their keys together preventing any from getting lost.

to *Carry It All*:

> With increasing concern for the environment, there is likely to be greater demand for carrying devices that can be used when travelling on foot or on public transport. Research carrying devices that already exist in different parts of the world, and use this information to design and make an environmentally friendly carrying device for someone in your local community.

They found out much more about the pupils' capabilities in the new short project than they had with the previous version. Adequate planning for differentiation or even setting could then be considered.

One teacher changed her approach to product evaluation. In the past pupils completed a pro forma sheet, which asked simple product analysis questions.

- What is it made from?

- Who is it for?

- When would it be used?

- Where is it used?

She kept these questions, but gave groups some optional questions on cards; these deliberately promoted high order thinking and were more probing, for example:

- What effect will this product have on people's lives?

- Is this a better product than . . .?

- What is wrong with this product?

- Why is this product not as popular as . . .?

- What could be done better or differently?

- What difficulties do users find with this product?

- Why have these particular ingredients been chosen?

- What else could have been used?

Another teacher included a new lesson with a focused task, 'Where do new design ideas come from?' He used information from designers and older pupils showing the pupils the stories of how their ideas emerged. They discussed the different approaches used, and he then encouraged the pupils to try out a range of strategies for generating new ideas, e.g. brainstorming; analysing products; using part of a visual image (window search); taking everyday objects and thinking up new uses for them (including outrageous ideas); observing changes as a result of fashion trends and lifestyle shifts; collecting images that inspired them. . . .

Using the level descriptions to identify exceptional performance

Teachers can use the National Curriculum in Action website (www.ncaction. org.uk) to identify pupils that are performing beyond their expected levels at entry to Key Stage 3.

National Curriculum D&T attainment target Levels 7 and 8 and exceptional performance

Level 7

Pupils use a **wide range** of appropriate sources of information to develop ideas. They investigate form, function and production processes before communicating ideas, using a variety of media. They recognise the **different needs of a range of users** and develop fully realistic designs. They produce plans that predict the time needed to carry out the main stages of making products. They work with a range of tools, materials, equipment, components and processes, taking full account of their characteristics. They **adapt** their methods of manufacture to changing circumstances, providing a sound explanation for any change from the design proposal. They select **appropriate techniques to evaluate** how their products would perform when used and modify their products in the light of the evaluation to **improve their performance**.

Level 8

Pupils use a **range of strategies to develop appropriate ideas**, responding to information they have identified. When planning, they **make decisions** on materials and techniques based on their understanding of the physical properties and working characteristics of materials. They **identify conflicting demands** on their design, explain how their ideas address these demands and use this **analysis** to produce proposals. They organise their work so that they can carry out processes accurately and consistently, and use tools, equipment, materials and components with precision. They identify a broad range of criteria for evaluating their products, clearly relating their findings to the purpose for which the products were designed and the appropriate use of resources.

Exceptional performance

Pupils **seek out** information to help their design thinking, and recognise the needs of a variety of client groups. They are **discriminating** in their selection and use of information sources to support their work. They work from formal plans that make the best use of time and resources. They work with tools, equipment, materials and components to a high degree of **precision**. They make products that are reliable and robust and that fully meet the **quality** requirements given in the design proposal.

Pupil-friendly interpretations of the level descriptions can be used to recognise performance beyond what is normally expected for Key Stage 3.

'Pupil-speak' level descriptions

(Paul Shallcross, Kent Advisory Service)

Level 7
I can . . .

- use a wide range of appropriate sources of information to develop my ideas
- research possible forms, functions and production techniques for my design
- communicate using a variety of media and techniques, e.g. models, mock-ups, orthographic/isometric/perspective drawings, and using ICT, e.g. '2D Design'
- consider the needs of a range of users, e.g. children aged 3–5, in my specification
- produce a fully realistic design
- annotate to show that I recognise 'conflicting' demands on my designs
- include the time needed for the main stages of making in my production plan
- understand the characteristics/properties of a range of materials, tools and processes (e.g. properties of acrylic, use of blender, effects/limitations of 'batik') and take account of these
- adapt my making to changing circumstances and explain these adjustments
- work out ways to test my product fully and evaluate against the specification
- adjust my product to improve it following evaluation.

Level 8
I can . . .

- use a range of strategies to develop appropriate ideas, responding to information I have identified
- when planning, make decisions on materials and techniques based on my understanding of the physical properties and working characteristics of materials
- identify conflicting demands on my design
- explain how my ideas address conflicting demands

- analyse the task and specification fully in order to produce proposals
- organise my work so that I can carry out processes accurately and consistently
- use tools, equipment, materials and components with precision
- identify a broad range of criteria for evaluating my products
- clearly relate my evaluation findings to the purpose for which the products were designed
- evaluate whether I have made appropriate use of resources.

Exceptional performance
I can . . .

- seek out information to help my design thinking, and recognise the needs of a variety of client groups
- be discriminating in my selection and use of information sources to support my work
- work from formal plans that make the best use of time and resources
- work with tools, equipment, materials and components to a high degree of precision.

An example of a pupil with exceptional performance – clock project

The project was about designing and manufacturing for a very specific market and how that brings new considerations and constraints to a designer.

A company is planning to produce a range of interesting artefacts, expressing cultural diversity from the past to the present. Design a clock using a standard mechanism, but explore a variety of appropriate techniques and finishes.

An exceptional performance response

Lucy produced a very comprehensive project, with all stages of the design process well documented. She discriminates in her selection and makes use of a wide range of appropriate sources of information on Chinese writing and images and on metals to develop her ideas, recognising the needs of client groups. She investigates form and function through her testing and texturing of metals. She communicates her initial ideas and design development using a variety of media, leading to a fully realistic working drawing. In 'plan of action' she tries to find the best use of time and resources when carrying out the main stages of production.

Lucy works with a range of tools, equipment, components and processes, demonstrating a high degree of precision through the careful use, marking out and cutting of material. She draws her chosen motif by hand, which was then scanned. She converts the image into a vector so that it could then be downloaded to a CAMM-1 machine, which plots the design onto vinyl.

Lucy adapts her methods of manufacture to changing circumstances as the design develops, for example changing the shape of the numbers to overcome problems when cutting them out.

She makes a reliable and robust product that fully met the quality requirements given in the design proposal. She selects appropriate techniques to evaluate how her clock would perform at various stages during production, and made modifications. For example, her review of material used for the 'turtle' design led her to use computer-aided manufacture (CAM) in order to improve performance.

Lucy's clock project

Using A grade examination descriptions

The awarding bodies' GCE and GCSE A grade descriptions may also give some characteristics (but probably not all) to be expected of the most able pupils at Key Stage 3.

Grade A design and technology: product design (2006 Advanced Subsidiary and Advanced examination)

Combining their designing and making skills with knowledge and understanding, candidates:

- when generating ideas and clarifying the task, use an **imaginative** range of appropriate primary research methods, analyse and record information and demonstrate a high degree of **selectivity**.
- when developing and communicating ideas, take into account functionality, aesthetics, ergonomics, maintainability, quality and user preferences, then work to a specification which could be developed in conjunction with an external partner or **client**. Take account of commercial manufacturing requirements in terms of scale of production, time and resource management. Demonstrate an understanding of product life cycles.
- Initiate and develop a wide range of **imaginative and feasible alternative ideas**, showing that they effectively and completely satisfy all of the specification criteria. Demonstrate **high level communication skills** through a wide variety of appropriate and effective methods and techniques, including information technology, graphical, numerical and linguistic
- when planning and evaluating, demonstrate good management of time and resources in the development of design proposals and appropriately test and evaluate final outcomes, as well as the various stages of development, **discriminating** between aspects which performed well and others which could be further improved. **Evaluate the effect of the design proposal upon the wider society**, taking into account, spiritual, moral, social, economic and environmental implications.
- when making, demonstrate demanding and high level skills which include shaping, forming, assembly and finishing, and show **imaginative use of materials**. Take into account quality assurance procedures and precise and appropriate levels of **tolerance** in the realisation of design proposals. Select, use

and demonstrate understanding of a range of materials/components and production processes appropriate to the specification and the scale of production. Demonstrate **high levels of safety awareness** both in the working environment and beyond.

Different types of most able pupils in D&T

In *Teaching the Very Able Child*, Wallace (2000) typified the characteristics of the very able pupil into three types – the very able high-flyer, the coaster and the disaffected. We have used these three categories to describe three quite different **able** pupils you may recognise in your D&T classrooms.

The very able high-flyer

Gemma loves learning new things. During her AS D&T project she decided to work in metal – she had very little experience of that before, as she previously specialised in textiles and had done textiles at GCSE. She was confident enough to know that she could try something new and untested for her project without jeopardising her marks. She's older than her years and shows good insights into how products will be used by people and their impact on a sustainable world. She relates well with adults and gets support from an extended network of family, friends, family work colleagues and local businesses. She works hard, is well organised in her project work and meets the deadlines that she needs to. The teachers and technicians find it easy to support Gemma and provide extra challenge for her. She gets a high mark in the examination.

The coaster

Raphe is the quiet one who is easy to overlook, completing all the pages for his coursework neatly and as required. D&T is mundane – a task or a series of tasks to get through. He doesn't like to interrupt the busy D&T teacher to ask questions – his questions always seem to be a bit odd compared with the rest of the class – best not to draw attention by saying something different. Often the teacher does not notice that he has finished – he's very good at making sure he looks busy by adding loads of annotations to his design drawings, drawing 15 colourways for the same design, or decorating his design sheets. If the teacher does notice that he's finished, he won't really want to complete any extension work, but will do, if pushed, with as little as he can get away with. Secretly, Raphe makes up loads of model kits at home, becomes absorbed in that activity, but would not share that interest with his teacher. He gets a high mark in his examination because he has completed all the required work, but it is still below his real potential.

The disaffected

Megan is a nightmare! She says that she hates D&T – it's 'boring' and that she is 'useless at it'. She can be uncooperative and confrontational – frequently disrupting lessons. As she moves from teacher to teacher on the carousel system her behaviour changes, and when the staff discussed her behaviour it became apparent that one teacher was having greater success than the others. It appeared that this teacher had a project that was a bit more creative than usual (she was piloting some of the Key Stage 3 National Strategy designing strategies for creativity). The teacher described how one activity involving role-plays and another involving generating ideas, quickly had engaged Megan. It is hard to predict what mark Megan will get in her exams; her coursework is incomplete, but her mock written paper exam score was excellent.

How to recognise and understand able underachievers

Constantly show interest. Don't allow them to stop doing work. Show them respect. Pass on older knowledge even if it is old fashioned or not used anymore – they don't make 'em like they used to. Give freedom to work.
(Dominic Johnson, Audi Young Designer finalist)

You could use this section as a department to clarify what the term 'able underachievers' means in D&T and to give everyone a chance to reflect on their practice:

- What and who are able underachievers in D&T?

- Why do some students underachieve in D&T?

- How can you identify them in D&T?

Think about the students that you've taught:

- How many of them have reached their true potential?

- How many underachieving students do you have in your class?

Consider why students underachieve

- Do some students choose not to reach their true potential?

- High ability students can sometimes have special social and emotional needs.

- Is there something happening in their life outside of school that affects their performance?

- Are some students less mature than others?

- Are there difficulties with peers because their ability sets them apart?

- Do the teachers have expectations based on experience with a sibling?

- Do the parents have high expectations and place pressure on the pupil?

- Does the pupil set high expectations of perfectionism for him/herself?

- Does the pupil feel anxious due to pressure being exerted on them?

- Does the pupil have poor social skills and feel isolated from his/her peers?

- Does the pupil have low self-esteem and does not believe in his/her own ability?

- Is the pupil unaware of his/her own potential?

- Does the pupil have difficulties in specific subjects and can this be due to cultural or gender issues of achievement?

- Has the pupil moved house or country recently?

- Has the pupil's family suffered a break-up?

- Is the pupil finding it difficult to cope with the transition between primary and secondary school?

Vulnerable groups

There are particular groups of students who are more vulnerable to underachievement than others, including:

- EAL – students who have English as an additional language

- students who have behavioural issues

- members of underachieving cultural minority groups

- gender issues with achievement with particular subjects

- disadvantaged able children

- gifted students with a learning difficulty.

When identifying students within your school, we need to ensure that the method of identification that we use actually does not allow students from vulnerable groups to be missed.

How would you characterise high ability in D&T?

One story that I always tell teachers is about a prizewinner at a YEDA/Young Engineering competition. This young teenager had come up with a new idea for brake lights on a standard car. His family had been involved in a rear-end shunt on the motorway and afterwards he wondered if it could have been prevented in some way. Even though he was years off being able to drive yet, he studied drivers' actions when they were braking and the braking systems. He noted that there was a significant time delay (milliseconds) from seeing the car ahead braking, to taking your foot off the accelerator and putting your foot on the brake to activate the brakes and the brake lights. He also noted that in an emergency braking situation, a driver takes their foot off the accelerator very fast. His design solution was to look differently at the problem and produce a sensor that sensed when your foot came off the accelerator quickly. This activated the brake lights milliseconds faster, but enough to save some serious car damage and maybe some lives . . . innovative, simple, clever . . . great idea!

What does this example show?

- freedom to investigate a problem of personal interest

- making a product that will make a real difference

- working in a context that was not familiar (driving)

- intervening creatively

- seeing and analysing what was happening in real life

- ethos of doing something different and taking risks

- questioning current systems and solutions

- curiousity, speculating, asking what if . . .?

- inventiveness

- not believing that established ways of doing things or adults have the right answer.

Why had nobody at BMW, Audi or Ford thought of this before? Think of James Dyson!

> 'But, James, if there were a better kind of vacuum cleaner Hoover or Electrolux would have invented it.'
>
> (G Coren, *James Dyson Against The Odds*, 1997: 1)

Characteristics of our most able inventors, designers, makers and engineers

What do inventive geniuses have in common? These creative minds all started with a vision and shared the traits of initiative, dedication, hard work, problem solving, courage, and perseverance. Their ideas have changed the world and the way we live our lives. Not only have their inventions touched every aspect of our daily living, but their personal qualities can be an inspiration for all.

(www.kyrene.org/schools/brisas/sunda/inventor/main.htm)

Here are some quotes and stories from a few of history's most innovative and creative thinkers. These words give us a glimpse into their personalities. Can you draw conclusions about personality traits based on these stories? What words come to mind when you read the words of these inventive geniuses?

Alexander Graham Bell

When one door closes another door opens; but we often look so long and so regretfully, upon the closed door that we do not see the ones which open for us.

George Washington Carver

How far you go in life depends on your being tender with the young, compassionate with the aged, sympathetic with the striving and tolerant of the weak and strong. Because some day in your life you will have been all of these.

George Carver was known in the US as the 'plant doctor'. He saw that many sweet potatoes and peanuts were going to waste because farmers grew too many of them. George did not like this. He locked his laboratory door and worked until he discovered 118 new ways to use sweet potatoes, including making flour, starch, sugar, molasses, vinegar, ink, dye and glue. He also discovered 300 new ways to use peanuts including washing powder, bleach, shoe polish, metal polish, ink, rubbing oil, cooking oil, axle grease, cattle feeds, thirty different dyes, a kind of plastic, shampoo, soap, shaving cream and the sacred peanut butter. He made linoleum and a sort of rubber from peanut shells.

When news of George's experiments came out, he became famous throughout America and England. Farmers loved the fact that all their sweet potatoes and peanuts had more uses, so they wouldn't waste their crops and could sell it all and make more money. His fame spread across the ocean too. George also invented many synthetics. One was synthetic marble made out of wood shavings.

Thomas Edison

Just because something doesn't do what you planned it to do doesn't mean it's useless.

Many of life's failures are people who did not realise how close they were to success when they gave up.

Opportunity is missed by most people because it is dressed in overalls and looks like work.

Genius is one per cent inspiration and ninety-nine per cent perspiration.

To invent, you need a good imagination and a pile of junk.

Results! Why man, I have gotten a lot of results. I know several thousand things that won't work.

Guglielmo Marconi – radio star

There cannot be many people who failed at school, did not go to university and then went on to win a Nobel Prize.

A lack of formal education, high-powered family connections and an unstoppable will to succeed helped Guglielmo Marconi to transmit the first radio signal across the Atlantic and launch the wireless-communications industry.

Marconi was not, by his own admission, any kind of scientist, or even much of an inventor. He did not make any fundamental discoveries and radio was mostly a matter of assembling parts created by other people, but his vision of the possibilities of communication and the unstoppable will to pursue it, were all his own. He applied the science and created a product for the world to see. And today, with Bluetooth wireless technology radio and 'wireless telegraphy' (texting), radio is centre stage again.

Pursuing an idea like that demanded the ability to move into a new world, not just optimise an old one. Marconi had this gift and was a true entrepreneur.

Apparently, at school, Marconi was not pressured into getting good grades and was allowed to follow his nose. His education was patchy; he never qualified for higher education, even with the help of a private physics tutor.

At the age of 20, Marconi worked hard in his parents' attic; he lashed together a Morse key, some batteries, an induction coil, a 'coherer' (a device for detecting radio waves), a big relay, and – his only personal invention – the all-important aerial and earth. He found he could send messages two kilometres, without wires and with a hill in the way. Marconi did not just throw all this stuff together. He was a tireless perfecter of small details.

And when he encountered problems in development, Marconi's lack of formal education proved an asset, for example when the physicists argued that there was no way that radio would work over the horizon. He never bothered to work things out; he just tried them. And in test after test he had already shown that radio did work, far beyond the horizon. By some means – identified later as reflection from the ionosphere – he could link places on either side of the hill of seawater caused by the curvature of the earth.

Trevor Baylis – inventor of the clockwork radio

In *Clock This* (1999), Trevor Baylis describes what it is like to be in the mind of an inventor who, inspired by a television documentary about HIV and AIDS in Africa, immediately took to his workshop and set to work on a radio that would work without electricity or batteries. His now world-famous invention sells at a rate of 120,000 a month. No mean feat for a man who described his early educational abilities as 'best suited to some form of early retirement'.

In pride of place above the toilet in his home on Eel Pie Island, London, Trevor Baylis has framed a letter from a fellow engineer outlining in detail why his idea of a clockwork radio would never work. Baylis takes great satisfaction from having proved him wrong.

After a childhood set against the backdrop of war-torn London – a veritable playground for Baylis and his buddies – and a life as an affluent teenager with £4 per week, an apprenticeship with a soil engineering firm and one day a week day-release to study for a certificate in engineering, Baylis quickly found his feet in the real world.

But there is much more to him than an engineering prodigy who struck lucky. Indeed, his life has to date been well and truly less ordinary. A world-class swimmer who narrowly missed qualifying for the Olympics, and who then, incredibly, found his fins by demonstrating swimming pools and later by flirting with the circus as a stuntman and underwater escapologist!

Trevor's infectious enthusiasm, dedication and humour have shone through every aspect of his life.

As long as you've got slightly more perception than the average wrapped loaf, you could invent something.

Isambard Kingdom Brunel – not just an engineer

www.brunel.ac.uk/news/events/team/ikbawards/whoisikb/

Isambard Kingdom Brunel exemplified the 'can do' Victorian culture. He grasped every chance that came his way, put 100% of effort into all his projects and, yes, he made some mistakes along the way (some were very expensive). But by taking risks, and being allowed to do so, he had fantastic triumphs too, which we are still using today.

Without doubt Brunel was an entrepreneur; he had the vision to see the product or service he wanted to create and was smart enough to solve the engineering problems to achieve his aim. In the face of severe opposition and much derision it was Brunel who recognised that steamships sailing from Bristol to New York would be a commercial winner – it was only afterwards that he worked out how to make it happen. But more than that, he had an eye for the dramatic – all of his designs were meant to grab your attention. IKB was not interested in the simply practical – it had to have style and panaché; whether a major bridge or a humble station building – all had to be aesthetically pleasing. And it wasn't just the items on show. His engineering solutions for lock gates, dry docks, or the internal structure of foundations and buttresses are simple and elegant, and they work better for it too. This vividly demonstrates just how well he understood physics and engineering, and meant that he could build longer, bigger, more boldly and cheaper, because he knew how to use materials to their best effect.

Brilliant as Brunel was, he had plenty of faults; not acknowledging others' efforts and work was one, and being utterly unreasonable in his demands of workmen and assistants, another. He was not an easy man to know, live with, or work for.

Beside the fact that he was an engineering genius, his pride in all aspects of his work is one of the main reasons why so many of his creations are with us today. But personally overseeing that construction was carried out to his exacting standards, spending long hours drawing up plans, coping with the pressure of getting calculations right, constantly having to innovate to solve problems, and keeping the commercial aspects in check took its toll. He died at the age of 53.

Beulah Henry

I cannot make up my mind whether it is a drawback or an advantage to be so utterly ignorant of mechanics as I am, I know nothing about mechanical terms and I am afraid I do make it rather difficult for the draughtsmen to whom I explain my ideas, but in the factories where I am known, they are exceedingly patient with me because they seem to have a lot of faith in my inventions.

Beulah Henry of Memphis, Tennessee, created about 110 inventions and held 49 patents. She was considered one of the 'Lady Edisons' for her prolific career in inventing including:

- vacuum ice cream freezer (1912)

- umbrella with a variety of different coloured snap-on cloth covers (1924)

- the first bobbinless sewing machine (1940)

- 'Protograph' – worked with a manual typewriter to make four copies of a document (1932)

- 'Continuously-attached Envelopes' for mass mailings (1952)

- 'Dolly Dips' soap-filled sponges for children (1929)

- 'Miss Illusion' doll with eyes that could change colour and close (1935).

Case studies of our most able pupils in D&T

Although the pupils in this section are post-16, their development and their observations provide useful insights for teachers of Key Stage 3 and Key Stage 4 pupils.

Jenny Andrews, 18, from Woldingham School

Characteristics

- Demonstrate high levels of technological understanding
- Rigorous analysis and interpretation of products
- High-quality making and precise practical skills
- Become irritated when a teacher demands that they follow a rigid design and make process

I realised that I had a particular talent in D&T because I enjoyed it lots when I was younger; I'd look forward to it. My projects used to be quite different from the others in the class and I loved the feeling of completing things I was proud of.

I have a wide range of skills, I think. I was good with wood at GCSE, I was also good at coming up with solutions to problems during manufacture and willing to try new processes such as welding and plasma cutters.

I've become more confident over recent years, I think partly due to my D&T teacher and experience where I have to justify and sell ideas to people. I don't tend to back down, which can lead me to become a bit tunnel visioned. I can be extremely focused if I find something I want.

Example project – Resistant materials: integral car jack for saloon cars

 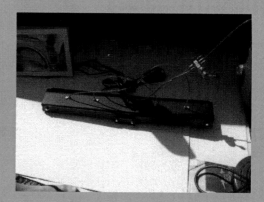

I was inspired to make this product from personal experience, because while driving last summer I got a flat tyre. This introduced me to the problems associated with jacking up a car on the roadside. As a result I chose to look into this problem area and try to resolve some of the issues I came across.

The first part of my research was to hand out a questionnaire to potential users to find out exactly what was needed. The next part led me to look at existing standard jacks and integral car jacks to see how previous products looked and had been made.

I have chosen to design and make an integral car jack (one that is permanently fixed onto the chassis of the car). My intention is for this device to lower and raise itself by the push of a button on the dashboard. This should reduce the length of time that the user, who is changing a tyre, is exposed to the dangers of the oncoming traffic on the roads etc. It would also reduce the inconvenience of having to empty out the boot to reach the car jack. By having it already in place there would be no need for the user to worry about getting it into the correct position, or the (sometimes) awkward job of using it by hand.

During my manufacturing stage I used a variety of processes. For example, to fold the metal sheets I had cut out using the plasma cutter, I used a large metal folder. I also used the lathe to turn my aluminium supports and make the brass bushes. I used the pillar drill on various components too.

Challenge and stretch

My teacher was very blunt; even if you were pleased with what you had done, he would still find problems. I was largely driven by wanting to please him. He lined up a meeting with Crudace Construction and got us involved with the Audi Young Designer Competition and let me have time out of school to visit companies.

Strategies that worked well for me:

- Criticism! Lists of what I needed to do. Long lists kicked me into action. I found I had to be very self-motivated in as much as the other two in my class hated D&T, so I would organise evenings to talk D&T theory in the run-up to the exam.

Ben Raffles, 17, St Albans School

Characteristics

- Flashes of inspiration, highly original or innovative ideas, different ways of working/approaches to issues
- Demonstrate high levels of technological understanding
- Rigorous analysis and interpretation of products
- High-quality making and precise practical skills
- Able to work comfortably in contexts beyond their own experience and empathise with users' and clients' needs and wants

I realised that I had a particular talent for D&T when I did fairly well at 14 years old. I made a kite buggy for GCSE when everyone made cupboards, and I got top marks in GCSE. I'm good at problem solving and overcoming design issues, and cope with all aspects of D&T. I'm a friendly, enthusiastic, quite addictive personality – if I do something I like to do it well!

Example project – Beach mobility aid

There are over 300 beaches in Britain alone, most of which have been engineered in various ways for the benefit of the public. However, most wheeled devices are not designed with beach use in mind; this includes wheelchairs and children's buggies. These tend to have four thin wheels, the front two of which are found to dig down into the sand, making pushing tiring, difficult and painful, with the risk of back injury if prolonged.

As society has evolved towards a more politically correct mentality, it is now a legal requirement for businesses and governments to provide access and equal rights to disabled people. In the US, an organisation called CRAB (Citizens Right to Access Beaches) fights for the facilities for disabled people to have access to beaches.

Currently, beach wheelchairs are available; however, they are very costly and designed for the widest possible market; as a result a 'one-size-fits-all' approach can result in discomfort for some.

The brief was to design an innovative, detachable and low-cost device that spreads the load of a wheelchair in order to cross soft terrain. To fulfil mass production requirements the product must also be suitable for any standard wheelchair without the need of modifications to the frame, thus reducing product cost and increasing potential profit.

After researching different types of all-terrain transport and methods of spreading load, I arrived at the conclusion to use a similar method as the Dyson

'Ball Barrow' (and since completion, the new vacuum cleaner) to relieve force on the front casters and a multiple wheel system to alleviate pressure on the rear wheels.

Challenge and stretch

My teacher encouraged me to take on more difficult projects. He allowed my classmates to make a cupboard or table and encouraged me to come up with an innovative product. He reacted very positively to me, helped after school to continue product work.

Strategies that worked well for me

- Never being allowed to take the easy option for a product.

Ruza Ivanovic, 18, from Shrewsbury Sixth Form College

Characteristics

- Flashes of inspiration, highly original or innovative ideas, different ways of working/approaches to issues
- Demonstrate high levels of technological understanding
- Sensitive to social and cultural issues when designing
- Rigorous analysis and interpretation of products
- High-quality making and precise practical skills
- Able to work comfortably in contexts beyond their own experience and empathise with users and clients needs and wants
- Become irritated when a teacher demands that they follow a rigid design and make process

I made a spaceship in Year 3; it was not so much a realisation of talent but a realisation of enjoyment. My strengths are researching in depth and applying practical solutions to problems, especially incorporating maths and physics. This is what I enjoy most. I tend to take an engineers' perspective. I am good across the range of D&T, though I have always found graphics very challenging. I struggle with graphic presentation – sketching, layout on page, rendering, etc.

By Year 7, I could:

- seek out information to help my design thinking
- recognise the needs of a variety of client groups
- discriminate in selecting and using information sources to support work
- work from formal plans that make the best use of time and resources
- work with tools, equipment, materials and components to a high degree of precision
- make products that are reliable and robust and that fully meet the quality requirements given in the design proposal.

[QCA description for exceptional performance at end of Key Stage 3, Year 9]

I enjoy several sports, mostly team ball games and I love to collaborate. I am particularly interested in mechanical engineering and relish a challenge.

Example project – Product design: micro-hydroelectricity

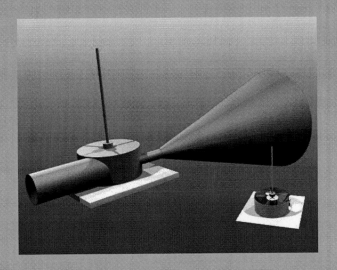

This project provided me with the opportunity to look at a challenging brief outside the normal realms of A Level study. It enabled me to incorporate my knowledge of maths and physics and confirmed my interest in mechanical engineering.

My design was influenced by the desire to develop independence within communities in Less Economically Developed Countries. Primarily, the system was designed to power a small, rural Kenyan flourmill, either directly or by producing electricity. However, the product also has the potential to be used in a wider context – it could be used in More Economically Developed Countries, such as the UK, to pump water for irrigation in allotments and smallholdings, for example.

During the research process I conducted two interviews – one with a chartered mechanical engineer and another with an employee at Dinorwig Hydroelectric plant in North Wales. I also used experimentation, theoretical and practical modelling, measurements of the speed of river flow in a local brook, several books (physics, design technology, hydroelectricity and engineering), informative displays at Dinorwig, class notes from GCSE and A Level maths and physics, e-mails from ITDG personnel, and some internet websites (including interactive material selection charts). Other research included looking into similar existing products (windmills, waterwheels and wind-up radios).

It was necessary to find out how a hydroelectric system works, the optimum size and shape of a turbine, flourmill machinery specifications, how to generate electricity and maximise power output, suitability and availability of materials, various anthropometrics and the scope for product application.

I used many different processes to manufacture the system, including 3D computer modelling (CAD), oxyacetylene welding, turning, drilling, parting/facing-off, riveting, vacuum forming, rolling and spot-welding. The micro-hydroelectric prototype worked successfully in trials with a comparably high efficiency rating.

Challenge and stretch

Chris Braden at Shrewsbury Sixth Form College has been an inspirational teacher. He was excellent. He pushed and stimulated me, helping me to find my strengths and interests. He really helped me to become aware of engineering. He set me different projects; he made me aware of developments and improvements. He helped me to realise ways to take my project further, for example to a higher, more thorough level. He gave up a lot of extra time to help me with challenges.

Strategies that worked well for me

- Freedom.

Julie Crawford, 18, from Grosvenor Grammar School

Characteristics

- Sensitive to aesthetic, social and cultural issues when designing
- Rigorous analysis and interpretation of products
- High-quality making and precise practical skills
- Able to work comfortably in contexts beyond their own experience and empathise with users' and clients' needs and wants

I'm good at a range of D&T areas. I'm good at working independently on coursework. I became good at making contacts with companies and experts for help and guidance. I enjoy paperwork for coursework and explaining my ideas. I'm not an expert with computers, so CAD programs were not easy for me to grasp, although I enjoyed sketching my initial ideas.

I was average at D&T at GCSE level, but the product design course at A Level suited me better, so I achieved higher marks. I always had a deep interest in the architecture aspects of design due to my dad's occupation.

I am very quiet by nature and technology has encouraged me to become more outspoken and confident when presenting my ideas. I am very hard-working and put my all into my work, continuously looking to improve it.

Example project – Emergency relief cot

My church has close connections with a village in Malawi; through talks on their work in the local hospital and community I identified the need for an inexpensive temporary cot, because overcrowding prevents adequate provision of facilities for newborn babies. Such a product would be beneficial for aid distribution following natural disasters like the Asian Tsunami, where all shelter is destroyed. The recent terrorist threats to airports with large volumes of passengers have resulted in many long stays in airport waiting areas. A lightweight emergency cot would provide a comfortable temporary bed for babies in extreme situations.

I researched the current market to ensure there were no existing products providing a gap in the market. I visited the Red Cross; they expressed a need for a suitable product meeting their specification. Internet research gave me the awareness of design possibilities created by cardboard engineering, and by visiting a packaging company I learnt about constraints placed on my design to ensure ease of mass production. When visiting an Ulster hospital, I was able to look at the design of the cot from a medical aspect, meeting the baby's needs and requirements, which therefore directly influenced my design.

The finished product will be designed using the principles of cardboard engineering. The product will then be drawn on CAD and manufactured through integrated CAM to ensure complete accuracy of measurements. Computer numerical control (CNC) systems are essential when mass-producing complex net shapes on a continuous production line. I hope to gain experience of the industrial scale of line production through close contact with SCA Packaging, as they provide advice and help creating the prototype product.

A designer's approach to any problem should be open-minded, resilient and forward thinking, showing awareness of issues such as technological push and market pull. Striving for imaginative solutions requires an awareness of constraints such as cost, methods of manufacture, environmental and user needs. A good designer should be willing to investigate new innovative technologies including the area of CAD/CAM and a range of CNC equipment. The use of creativity and imagination coupled with an understanding of business strategies are essential characteristics to ensure the design of intuitive and inventive products.

Challenge and stretch

The teachers were very helpful, giving up a lot of time to help me and encouraging me to enter competitions. They helped me reach my potential, helping me make contact with lots of experts and companies to ensure a high-quality project and product. The teachers stayed after school, so the schools' facilities were available to use.

Strategies that worked well for me

- Making contact with very helpful people in industry and business, who helped me make full use of their resources
- I enjoy the coursework aspect and find it less stressful than sitting exams.

Emily Cummins, 18, from South Craven School

Characteristics

- Flashes of inspiration, highly original or innovative ideas, different ways of working/approaches to issues
- Demonstrate high levels of technological understanding
- Sensitive to aesthetic, social and cultural issues when designing

- Rigorous analysis and interpretation of products
- High-quality making and precise practical skills
- Able to work comfortably in contexts beyond their own experience and empathise with users' and clients' needs and wants
- Become irritated when a teacher demands that they follow a rigid design and make process

When I was three or four years old I used to help my granddad in his hut. We made toys and I got a hammer as a gift. I haven't looked back since then!

Ideas are my strong point and then making them. I am a perfectionist; I don't stop until it's at the level I want it to be at. I am good across a range of D&T areas, good on theory and research. I love the research as it gives and generates hundreds of ideas. I research until I can't anymore, because of time.

By the end of primary school and Year 7, I could:

- seek out information to help my design thinking
- recognise the needs of a variety of client groups
- work from formal plans that make the best use of time and resources
- work with tools, equipment, materials and components to a high degree of precision
- make products that are reliable and robust and that fully meet the quality requirements given in the design proposal.

[These points concur with the QCA description for exceptional performance at the end of Key Stage 3, Year 9]

I find drawing very difficult, but I am trying to learn now. I love working in teams, but people tend to let me be in control. Even though we do work in teams I have learnt from business, motivation and leadership, skills that make teamwork more fun. I am very confident and I feel I am very able in communicating ideas and talking to people. I am also very organised and have good motivational skills.

Example project – Product design: sustainable refrigerator

Whilst attending the National Design Sustainability Awards I was shocked at how big a problem global warming has become; this is due to the rate at which fossil fuels are being burnt. Everyday appliances cannot be used 'every day' for much longer.

After extensive research I found that the refrigerator was the main appliance that people did not want to live without; therefore, I decided to design and make a prototype of a sustainable refrigerator.

I have performed various scientific tests to find the most suitable sustainable materials to use, taking into account: efficient function, the amount of energy used to produce the materials, availability and cost.

I am using aluminium for the outer casing of my design, because it is easy to recycle and uses low energy to produce. I have needed to use TIG welding to join sections of the casing together and I have even looked into the technique of raising. My final product is a full working model; its size would be perfect for transporting medicines, but my design could also be manufactured on a larger scale, as the theory would still work.

My design reduces the amount of fossil fuels being burnt now, but in the future it could be used as a refrigeration unit when we totally run out of fossil fuels. With some slight tweaking my fridge will be suitable for use in developing countries too.

Challenge and stretch

I was the strongest in my class and teachers used to ask me to explain answers to the class. Some classmates were jealous, but others were really happy saying that they want to keep in touch with me because one day I will be famous – it makes me laugh!

The teachers treated me differently to everyone else. They gave me more respect and more attention. Teachers went to businesses outside of school, and companies that offered help, for example ITDG (now Practical Action); I was asked to complete the Sustainable Design Award, which increased my product depth.

Strategies that worked well for me

- Working alongside companies. The businesses that were specific to the product that I was making, allowed me to gain more knowledge as people were extremely talented in this area and really helped me.

Sam Mitcham, 18, from Hereford Sixth Form College

Characteristics

- Flashes of inspiration, highly original or innovative ideas, different ways of working/approaches to issues
- Demonstrate high levels of technological understanding
- High-quality making and precise practical skills
- Become irritated when a teacher demands that they follow a rigid design and make process

I've always been good at the practical side of things and finding solutions to problems. I always want to take on interesting projects that are too big for the given time. I don't think I have a special talent in D&T, so to speak; I just applied myself to something I enjoyed. I think if you want something bad enough you can achieve it.

Did my test and exam results, and the marks allocated give me credit for my strengths? Not in the slightest – I really don't seem to get on with the curriculum when it comes to D&T and Art. I much prefer the way that competitions (like Audi Young Designer) are run and what they look for.

Example project – Mountain bike four cross frame

My aim was to design a mountain bike four cross frame that will allow a greater level of competition riding to be reached without compromise. The current Four Cross frames are either pedal efficient or suspension efficient, but not both to the degree they could be.

The design incorporates the stiffness and pedal efficiency of a Unified rear triangle design with the rear suspension activeness of a single pivot or linkage design, something that has not yet been developed into one single frame design. As a confident competitive rider myself, I can see a great need for a frame that incorporates these ideas and works.

The design has been thoroughly researched and evaluated to the point where a fully working prototype has been produced and tested. The research identified several important issues that have been addressed; these include the design of a frame that is not only pedal-efficient, active and strong, but is also light and whippy to ride. The frame must also have a suitable weight distribution at both extended and compressed suspension levels, to enable effective high-speed cornering, jumping and control.

My frame is produced mainly from chromoly steel tubing, making it incredibly strong; however, thinner gauge tubing will keep weight to a minimum. The rear suspension will be handled by a Fox Float R rear suspension unit, suitable for the type of riding the frame is intended for, and the rear end will pivot smoothly on four individual cartridge bearings.

Challenge and stretch

My teachers suddenly realised that I wasn't just a pretty face!

Strategies that worked well for me

- It's brilliant when everyone wants to achieve something, when everyone is bouncing off one another, like at an event such as a '24-hour Challenge'.

Dominic Johnson, 17, from Heaton Manor School

Characteristics

- Flashes of inspiration, highly original or innovative ideas, different ways of working/approaches to issues
- Demonstrate high levels of technological understanding
- Rigorous analysis and interpretation of products
- High-quality making and precise practical skills
- Become irritated if a teacher demanded that they follow a rigid design and make process

You either **do** D&T or you **don't**. With most of my friends it is all or nothing, even if their all won't get them a high grade (if one at all).

I am good at creating and developing concepts – new and old. I have a wide knowledge of general manufacturing processes; I am very logical in problem solving and product development. I was good in most areas of D&T, apart from communicating ideas. I didn't take Art at GCSE or A level, so drawings and images put down on the page were more difficult than tangible models or prototypes. I could visualise an idea, explain it, but not accurately commit it to paper.

My exam results did not give me as much credit for my strengths as I would have liked. Grades aren't as important to me as achievements. I feel you can still achieve a great deal without a good grade.

I'm a bit of a workaholic on D&T projects; I'm active, constantly wanting to improve, involved, busy, tired!

Example project – D&T systems and control: Karmalight

One of the most relaxing lighting effects that I have seen is one created by a swimming pool where sunlight is refracted and patterns are created by the random movement of the surface water.

I have tried to re-create this effect. To do this, I have investigated the use of readily available fluids, such as water, oil, spirits, etc. having different densities and viscosities. I have used electronics to move the fluid in a clear tank and also have other customisations for the light. Once I found out, and researched, what basic components were required, I created designs around them that would give the effect I was looking for. I investigated various electrical components such as PICs (Programmable Integrated Circuits), output circuitry, as well as current amplifiers – relays, transistors, etc. and RCDs (Residual Current Devices).

Manufacturing processes during the fabrication of the product include:

- laser cutting to develop a Perspex lens for a set of three LEDs
- soldering in the manufacture of PCBs.

I also wrote programs for PICs circuits to control the effect created by the product.

This final product design brings together all of the concepts that I have developed through research, for each element of the Karmalight, which more than satisfies the requirements of the original project brief.

For example, the LED lens shows off the product as a static object and also adds kinetic patterns.

The natural wooden base provides a traditional element which, when combined with the steel outer casing, creates a modern, yet familiar product. The Perspex clips at the top break up the long tubular design and add interest, whilst the halogen and filter levels, together with the Pyrex bowl enable this light to achieve the intended calming upward projection of fluid colour.

Challenge and stretch

I had three teachers. I saw them all, once a week each. They all added something to the close-knit atmosphere in some way. There was a lot of freedom in the selection of projects; we could select an easy or a hard project – anything we wanted within reason.

The class were like a family of brothers – without the fighting – constantly helping each other; we created a perfect working atmosphere and the teachers played the 'bigger brother' of the group, joining in on a very regular basis.

Strategies that worked well for me

- I constantly choose challenging, difficult and complex projects
- Practical lessons.

Jack Spencer, 18, from Alton College

Characteristics

- Flashes of inspiration, highly original or innovative ideas, different ways of working/approaches to issues
- Demonstrate high levels of technological understanding
- Sensitive to aesthetic, social and cultural issues when designing
- Rigorous analysis and interpretation of products
- High-quality making and precise practical skills
- Able to work comfortably in contexts beyond their own experience and empathise with users' and clients' needs and wants

In D&T I'm good at the practical design and manufacture. I'm particularly good at design, mechanisms, creating simple but effective designs and prototyping. But I do struggle with electronics. I used to love prototyping little inventions in my shed and realised that I had a particular talent in D&T when I was 10 years old. I do not think that the test and exam results gave me credit for my strengths in D&T. I'm active, creative, easy-going, motivated and reliable.

Example project – Product design: Kite Landboard

The design has been developed over about eight months through a great deal of research, initial ideas, further development and a series of prototypes. The product is to be used in conjunction with a powerful kite that provides propulsion, both across the ground and into the air. Therefore, it was imperative to develop a product that could be stable at speed as well as being suitable for freestyle use.

My design is unique in that the steering system is previously unheard of and completely radical. It relies upon the flex of the carbon fibre that comprises the deck to work. The deck is split into two pieces and with a series of restricted pivots the board is steered like any other board, but with weight and stability advantages. A patent application has been filed and companies are showing an interest to sort out a deal with me for the rights to produce and sell the idea.

Challenge and stretch

My teacher responded well to me, very supportive. I challenged myself with my project. I did not need challenging further. Providing extracurricular classes, free access to the workshop when open, advice and making sure you don't stifle creativity, helps.

Strategies that worked well for me

- Free access to the workshop.

INSET activities to develop the D&T department's ability to recognise and plan for the most able pupils

What to do:

1. Make copies of the checklists of characteristics of the most able (on the CD).

2. In a pair, discuss which characteristics you have seen in the most able pupils that you have taught. If you have staff new to teaching you could discuss the case studies in this chapter instead.

3. In a pair, discuss the lists and start to list characteristics of the most able in D&T and ways that these might be observed in D&T.

4. As a department share your lists, combine and agree on a departmental checklist of characteristics to add to your departmental handbook.

CHAPTER 4

Giftedness and learning difficulties

> . . . if they don't 'tick your boxes', if they confuse, irritate and question then don't write them off. Design isn't about conforming.
>
> (Wayne Hemingway, www.hemingwaydesign.co.uk)

When identifying and working with gifted and talented pupils, care needs to be taken to ensure that all pupils who are able in design and technology are identified and that appropriate provision is made for them, regardless of their gender, ethnicity or socioeconomic class. Cultural differences, language problems and peer expectations may influence performance and make recognition of pupils who are able in design and technology, difficult.

Some pupils, who are both gifted and learning disabled, exhibit remarkable talents or strengths in some areas and disabling weaknesses in others. They largely fall into three categories:

1. identified gifted pupils who have subtle learning disabilities

2. unidentified pupils whose gifts and disabilities may be masked by average achievement

3. identified learning disabled pupils who are also gifted.

Identified gifted pupils who have subtle learning disabilities

This group is easily identified as gifted because of high achievement or high IQ scores. As they grow older, discrepancies widen between expected and actual performance. These pupils may impress teachers with their verbal abilities, while their spelling or handwriting contradicts the image. At times, they may be forgetful, sloppy and disorganised. At Key Stage 4 where there are more, longer coursework projects and a heavier emphasis on researching, reading and written evaluations, some bright pupils find it increasingly difficult to achieve. Concerned adults are convinced that if these pupils would only try harder, they could succeed.

While increased effort may be required for these pupils, the real issue is that they simply do not know how! They are likely to be overlooked for screening procedures necessary to identify a subtle learning disability. It is important that these pupils do not go unrecognised as this would help pupils understand why they are experiencing academic difficulties and teachers could offer learning strategies and techniques to help them deal with their duality of learning behaviours.

However, a learning disability is not the only cause of a discrepancy between potential and achievement, as the section on able underachievers on p. 41 explains.

Unidentified pupils

Some pupils for a variety of reasons are not noticed at all. These pupils struggle throughout lessons to keep up. In essence, their gift masks the disability and the disability masks the gift. Their hidden talents and abilities may emerge in specific content areas or may be stimulated by a classroom teacher who uses a creative approach to learning. The disability is frequently discovered in adulthood when they happen to read about dyslexia, dyspraxia or Asperger syndrome and recognise some of the things that they struggled with in childhood.

Identified learning disabled pupils who are also gifted

These bright pupils, who are identified as 'learning disabled', are often failing miserably in school. They are first noticed because of what they cannot do, rather than because of the talent they are demonstrating. Because these pupils are bright and sensitive, they are more acutely aware of their difficulty in learning. Their schooling focuses on their problems, rather than their strengths and interests. In failing, they feel inadequate. But, they often have high-level interests at home. They will tell you about fantastic models or structures they have made. The creative abilities, intellectual strength and passion they bring to their hobbies are clear indicators of their potential for giftedness. Research has shown that teachers often rate this group of pupils as most disruptive at school. They are frequently found to be off-task; they may act out, daydream, or complain of headaches and stomachaches; and they are easily frustrated and use their creative abilities to avoid tasks.

Particular efforts also need to be made to ensure that pupils with disabilities who are talented in design and technology are identified and that appropriate provision is made to assist them in overcoming difficulties and developing their abilities.

- Pupils who are 'hearing impaired' may lack vocabulary and linguistic skills and have difficulty in responding to oral questions or expressing themselves in a way that reflects the complexity of their thoughts.

- Visual impairment may result in particular problems with work relating to developing their practical skills.

- Pupils who have specific learning difficulties may experience difficulties in planning and organising their work, but may have good problem solving skills.

Design and technology teachers need to work closely with special educational needs teachers to ensure that talents are identified and suitable curriculum provision is made for all able pupils.

A useful checklist ('Dual Exceptionalities' by Colleen Willard-Holt (1999)) is on the CD that accompanies this book. The checklist includes characteristics of gifted pupils with specific disabilities, for example:

- gifted students with visual impairment

- gifted students with physical disabilities

- gifted students with hearing impairments

- gifted students with learning disabilities.

It also includes:

- characteristics of gifted pupils who are bored

- characteristics of pupils with attention deficit hyperactivity disorder (ADHD)

- questions to ask in differentiating between giftedness and ADHD.

Examples of design and technologists with learning difficulties

We sometimes think negatively of a learning difficulty such as dyslexia. It is important for D&T teachers to recognise that some learning difficulties contribute to pupils D&T capability in quite remarkable ways. Ofsted often report that pupils with SEN make more progress in D&T than any other subject. The hands-on creative, problem solving, open-ended 3D nature means that pupils excel in this subject where they might struggle in maths, English, languages and humanities. There are a number of well-known designers and technologists who have admitted learning difficulties. Far from hampering their success, sometimes their condition has contributed to their gift.

Here are some examples of people with profound intellectual disabilities, such as autism, dyslexia, ADHD, and dyspraxia who have a 'fragment of genius' in D&T.

Autism (including Asperger syndrome)

Autism is a lifelong developmental disability. It is a spectrum disorder occurring in varying degrees of severity and affects more than an estimated 500,000 people in the UK. It is characterised by a triad of impairments, which involve difficulties forming social relationships, problems with verbal and non-verbal communication and problems with imagination. Asperger syndrome is frequently linked with giftedness.

Martin

Those of you who have been around me a lot have noticed that sometimes I act like I'm from another planet. I may flap my hands, or not look at you when I talk, or not understand your hints or body language. Things you think are nothing may really upset me, and things you can ignore may distract me from the job at hand. I have trouble following a long string of instructions, but I can get so involved in a book that I don't realise I'm in a room full of active, noisy people ... This gives me advantages and disadvantages. On the good side, I can be unbelievably smart at some things, like remembering different computer codes, or remembering dates and facts and trivia, or having different formulas for getting the right answers to math problems. I can read technical books written for adults, and 'talk shop' with people at Dad's computer lab at work, sometimes even helping them solve programming problems.

On the bad side, I am prone to asthma, allergies and thyroid problems. My muscles aren't strong or coordinated, I have trouble working in groups and bullies use me as an easy target. I can't keep my desk and folders organised, I really hate being outdoors, and certain clothes just don't feel right and bug me to death. And sometimes, I just get overloaded and need to get away for a few minutes to find my centre again.

I'm not asking you to feel sorry for me. Because if you pity me, you are also pitying all the great people like me, for example: Thomas Edison, Alexander Graham Bell and Shatoshi Tijjaru (creator of Pokemon), who all have autistic traits.

We're not looking for a cure for Asperger's – just your understanding, and the understanding that comes from research. After all, if autism were cured, society would lose access to many of its great geniuses and inventors. We need you to accept us and be friends with us, while we learn to survive and be successful in your world.

(from *Fitting In and Speaking Out: Me and Asperger's Syndrome*, on the Hoagies' Gifted Education Page website: www.hoagiesgifted.org/fitting_in.htm)

There are some remarkable examples of individuals who have extraordinary specific abilities (drawing, memory, calculating) while being extremely limited in all others. One example is Stephen Wiltshire, who was taught by my colleague for a time at Wood Lane School. Stephen has a remarkable talent for drawing, which has made him very successful in his life (he is now a professional full-time artist). He also has perfect pitch and is musically gifted. At school, he was very fond of the practical side of food technology and later signed up for catering college.

Stephen Wiltshire

Stephen Wiltshire was born in London to West Indian parents in 1974. As a child, Stephen was mute and did not relate to other human beings. Aged three, he was diagnosed as autistic. He had no language, uncontrolled tantrums and lived entirely in his own world. At the age of five, Stephen was sent to Queensmill Special School where the teachers could not fail to notice that he enjoyed drawing – animals, buses, buildings. His drawings were extraordinarily mature, showing a natural gift for perspective and ability to remember and reproduce the detail in each structure.

When he was 13 years old he was featured on the BBC QED programme, 'The Foolish Wise Ones', where Sir Hugh Casson (past president of the Royal Academy), described him as 'the best child artist in Britain'.

Stephen is the only artistic autistic savant in the world whose work has been recorded and published since his childhood and has appeared on numerous TV programmes. His third book – Floating Cities (Michael Joseph, 1991) – was number one on the Sunday Times bestseller list.

In 2003, thousands went to a gallery in Twickenham, London, to see the first major retrospective of Stephen's work, from 1983 to 2003, with 150 examples of drawings, paintings and prints.

(from www.stephenwiltshire.co.uk)

It has often been said that savants have photographic or eidetic memories, but as I photocopied Stephen's drawings I thought how unlike a Xerox machine he was. His pictures in no sense resembled copies or photographs, something mechanical and impersonal – there were always additions, subtractions, revisions, and, of course, Stephen's unmistakable style. They were images and showed us some of the immensely complex neural processes that are needed to make a visual and graphic image. Stephen's drawings were individual constructions, but could they be seen, in a deeper sense, as creations?

(Dr Oliver Sacks, An Anthropologist on Mars: Seven Paradoxical Tales, Picador, 1995)

Recently, scientists in Australia and the US think they have identified the part of the brain (left arterial temporal lobe), which if switched off, can stimulate artistic genius and they believe that ordinary people may one day be able to 'tap in' and allow them at least a moment of genius. They think that when a specific part of the brain does not work properly, abilities in another area may be unlocked and that the savants have their gifts, because of this 'malfunction' of the brain, not in spite of it.

For example, Stephen Wiltshire is taken up in a helicopter over London. Hours later, he produces a detailed and accurate drawing of a four-square-mile area of the City. The scientists believe this is possible because instead of his brain processing details of information, such as identifying a building or recognising it, he can tune in to all the complex mental processes that lie behind that recognition, and copy them.

ADHD

ADHD is a label used to describe certain characteristics including an apparent inability to concentrate. Pupils of high ability often fail to concentrate, and exhibit a kind of energy called 'hyperactivity'. But if you observe that the ability to concentrate exists in a child, the 'attention deficit' cannot be a root element of the character. To a certain extent, lack of concentration in very able pupils often results from the fact that the material is banal, repetitive or of a low level.

> Profound statements roll from his mouth, much too mature and intellectual for a child of his age. He remembers experiences you've long since forgotten and drags you to the window to watch the raindrops, falling like diamonds from the sky. On the good days being the parent of a spirited child is astounding, dumbfounding, wonderful, funny, interesting, and interspersed with moments of brilliance.
>
> (Mary Sheedy Kurchinka, Raising Your Spirited Child, 1998)

Pupils with ADHD can be gifted in D&T, as they often have a creative problem solving approach that does not always follow the normal 'rules'. As one ADD adult writes:

> I find that when 'normal' people are faced with a challenging issue or crisis or problem – they start thinking of all the ins and outs and how to go about solving the problem and all the reasons why or why not they should do what they want to do. Then after all that they start thinking of all the different ways they can go about doing what they decided they are going to do. All this takes time. Me, I just jump into something headfirst. I don't think according to rules and guidelines and . . . And most of the time people say 'wow – how did you think of that?' It does cause trouble sometimes. But most of the time it works to my advantage . . .
>
> (Goldie)

How can teachers distinguish between ADHD and giftedness?

Seeing the difference between behaviours that are sometimes associated with giftedness but also characteristic of ADHD is not easy, as the following parallel lists shows.

However, there are subtle differences. Gifted pupils do not exhibit problems in all situations, for example their behaviour can be different from one teacher to another. By contrast, pupils with ADHD typically exhibit the problem behaviours in virtually all settings, including at home and at school.

A gifted pupil's perceived inability to stay on task is likely to be related to boredom, curriculum, mismatched learning style, or other environmental factors. Gifted pupils may spend 20–50% of class time waiting for others to catch up and as a result become involved in 'off-task' behaviour and disruptions.

Hyperactive is a word often used to describe gifted pupils as well as pupils with ADHD. Pupils with ADHD have a high-activity level, but this activity level is often found across situations. Gifted pupils can be highly active too, but their

Behaviours associated with ADHD	Behaviours associated with giftedness
• Poorly sustained attention in almost all situations	• Poor attention, boredom, daydreaming in specific situations
• Diminished persistence on tasks not having immediate consequences	• Low tolerance for persistence on tasks that seem irrelevant
• Impulsivity, poor delay of gratification	• Judgement lags behind development of intellect
• Impaired adherence to commands to regulate or inhibit behaviour in social contexts	• Intensity may lead to power struggles with authorities
• More active, restless than normal pupils	• High activity level; may need less sleep
• Difficulty adhering to rules and regulations	• Questions rules, customs and traditions
(from Barkley 1990)	(from Webb *et al.* 1982)

activity is generally focused and directed. They can concentrate for long periods of time on whatever truly interests them. Their specific interests may not coincide, however, with their teachers' demands.

One characteristic of ADHD, which is distinctive, is that pupils with ADHD tend to be highly inconsistent in the quality of their performance and the amount of time used to accomplish tasks.

Determining whether a pupil has ADHD can be particularly difficult when that pupil is also gifted. The use of many instruments, including intelligence tests administered by qualified professionals, achievement and personality tests, as well as parent and teacher rating scales, can help the professional determine the subtle differences between ADHD and giftedness.

(Adapted from James T Webb and Diane Latimer, *ERIC EC Digest #E522,* 1993, ericec.org/digests/e522.html.)

Dyslexia

. . . dyslexic people are visual, multi-dimensional thinkers. [Dyslexics] are intuitive and highly creative, and excel at hands-on learning. Because we think in pictures, it is sometimes hard for us to understand letters, numbers, symbols and written words. We can learn to read, write and study effectively when we use methods geared to our unique learning style.

(*Dyslexia – the Unwrapped Gift* video)

Many very able pupils are 'dyslexic' to some degree (but it is possible that more than 50% of the population have some dyslexic characteristics!). Humans communicate through symbols (speech, written words, signs) and our ability to learn to encode and decode these symbols into meaningful ideas cannot be traced to a specific organ, but is wrapped up in the complexities of neurological brain development. The links between us understanding how our brains work and how we should teach reading and writing are strong. Not everyone is going to learn in the same way! It is not clear that dyslexia is intrinsically a defect. It may offer an alternative way of seeing, almost providing a 'three-dimensional' viewpoint in some instances. Of course, this is not very helpful when a two-dimensional activity like writing is required. Again, it is not always helpful to regard this condition as some kind of 'disease'. Some, perhaps all, dyslexic pupils gain by being 'dyslexic', though what they gain may not always be acceptable to the educational world.

More specific information can be obtained from The Dyslexia Association, www.bdadyslexia.org.uk.

For some designers and technologists dyslexia has provided a different viewpoint and with this has emerged some of our greatest thinkers and inventors.

Two qualities in dyslexics are outstanding:

- the understanding/awareness/management of 3D form and space

- the understanding/awareness/management of innovative composition.

Albert Einstein, Thomas Edison and Leonardo Da Vinci all suffered from early learning disabilities, centring on memory difficulties and limited abilities in reading, retention and recall. To compensate for and overcome left brain weaknesses in verbal retention and reading/writing, these great inventors significantly developed their right brain strengths of visualisation and detailed patterning, leading to discoveries that have changed the study and nature of physics, provided numerous day-to-day electrical applications and altered the very way we view our world.

Albert Einstein

He told me that his teachers reported that . . . he was mentally slow, unsociable, and adrift forever in his foolish dreams.

(Hans Albert Einstein, on his father, Albert Einstein)

Thomas Edison

My teachers say I'm addled . . . my father thought I was stupid, and I almost decided I must be a dunce.

Tommy Hilfiger, fashion designer

I performed poorly at school, when I attended, that is, and was perceived as stupid because of my dyslexia. I still have trouble reading. I have to concentrate very hard at going left to right, left to right, otherwise my eye just wanders to the bottom of the page.

I didn't want anyone to know that I didn't get it. [In reference to his being the class clown.]

Marco Pierre White, chef and restaurateur

Like many people with a handicap, I compensated elsewhere. When I had difficulty with spelling and reading, I concentrated on mathematics and sports. However back in class, I found traditional teaching methods such as standing up and reading aloud in class pure torture. Dyslexia gave me a different way of looking at things. A compulsion to dissect ideas and concepts from every possible angle has stayed with me.

Robert Rauschenberg, artist

The possibility always exists to nourish an important new genius in learning-disabled pupils, if their spirit is not broken and creative dreams are allowed to develop.

Jørn Utzon, architect

The Sydney Opera House, designed by Jørn Utzon (© 2006 Jupiterimages Corporation)

Richard Branson, founder of Virgin Enterprises

Richard didn't breeze through school. It wasn't just a challenge for him – it was a nightmare. His dyslexia embarrassed him, as he had to memorise and recite word for word in public. He was sure he did terribly on the standard IQ tests . . . these are tests that measure abilities where he is weak. In the end, it was the tests that failed. They totally missed his ability and passion for sports. They had no means to identify ambition, the fire inside that drives people to find a path to success that zigzags around the maze of standard doors that won't open. They never identified the most important talent of all. It's the ability to connect with people – mind to mind, soul to soul. It's that rare power to energise the ambitions of others so that they, too, rise to the level of their dreams.

Ironically, Richard Branson's talents began to show themselves during his adolescent school years. Frustrated with the rigidity of school rules and regulations, and seeing the energy of pupil activism in the late 1960s, he decided to start his own pupil newspaper. This might not have been remarkable, except that this paper was intended to tie many schools together. It would be focused on the pupils and not the schools. It would sell advertising to major corporations. It would have articles by Ministers of Parliament, rock music stars, intellectuals and movie celebrities. It would be a commercial success.

(Adapted from www.johnshepler.com/articles/branson.html.)

William Hewlett, co-founder, Hewlett-Packard

Hewlett was hampered by undiagnosed dyslexia, which gave him difficulty with written assignments, but led him to develop exceptional memorisation and logical skills. Hewlett excelled in mathematics and sciences. (obits.com/ hewlettwilliam.html)

Craig McCaw, telecommunications visionary

'Growing up, I had trouble fitting in,' said Mr McCaw in a 1998 interview. 'As a dyslexic, I don't think like other people, so I didn't fit very well in a clique.'

Mr. McCaw is shy and unassuming, visibly uncomfortable during his rare public speaking engagements. The narrative of his ideas is disjointed, his point only becomes clear when his trains of thought collide in an unpredicted conclusion. He is famously well-known for blowing the punch-lines of jokes.

But it is important to understand how his dyslexia has influenced significantly his entrepreneurial vision. Mr. McCaw credits his ability to see circumstances from unique perspectives – to see, for example, the potential of cellular communications, an insight that seems obvious now but that was uncommon in its day – to the challenges of growing up dyslexic. 'Dyslexia forced me to be quite conceptual, because I'm not very good at details,' he said at his 1997 induction into the Academy of Achievement. 'And because I'm not good at details, I tend to be rather spatial in my thinking—oriented to things in general terms, rather than the specific. That allows you to step back and take in the big picture. I feel blessed about that.'

(www.thealarmclock.com/magazine/magContent/mccaw.htm)

Paul Orfalea, founder of Kinko's

In my investment strategies class, my teacher almost failed me because I made so many spelling errors on his tests. When he found out I had learning difficulties, he announced to the class that I was 'on the brink of brilliancy' because he looked at my ideas instead of the spelling. The pupils were impressed after that, and they thought I saw the world a little differently.

Charles Schwab, investor

'Along the way, I've frustrated some of my associates because I could see the end zone of a particular thing quicker than they could, so I was moving ahead to conclusions,' he said. 'I go straight from step A to Z, and say: "This is the outcome. I can see it."'

Sally Shaywitz, director of the Learning Disorders Unit at Yale University, says that Schwab's ability to see solutions that others cannot is typical of dyslexics: 'What distinguishes them is that they really think outside of the box. Dyslexics often have a variety of qualities, including resilience, adaptability and the ability to formulate original insight.'

Thomas West and Daniel Sandin

Both Thomas and Daniel have dyslexia and are incredibly creative. West is the author of *In the Mind's Eye: Visual Thinkers, Gifted People with Learning Difficulties, Computer Imaging, and the Ironies of Creativity*. Daniel Sandin is a professor in Chicago University's School of Art and Design. He is a pioneer in virtual reality development.

West says that dyslexic people are often highly visual, able to quickly process and integrate high-quality visual and spatial information.

> Society is shifting with far more call for that sort of skill than for more mechanical tasks like reading and writing.

People with dyslexia seem to problem-solve in unusual ways, perhaps working from the inside out or from the back to the front. Sandin, who says he still cannot spell or do arithmetic, talks about developing the CAVE virtual reality system, which uses rear projection screens instead of a headset and knows where you are by generating your position in the room. It is a visual simulator completely matched to the human visual perceptual capability, he says.

> The dyslexic person may well be at the fore as the technological revolution continues, with their ability to process information and data and depict visually creating 'a whole new literacy.'

Specialised toolkits for dyslexic designers – STIK

How do you take a dry, prescribed written brief and transform it into a process that assists dyslexic designers to explore, analyse and capture their ideas at every stage of design development and then play them back?

STIK is a toolkit by Corporate Edge to help dyslexics when designing and making, to take briefs, capture ideas and arrive at solutions. It is a winner at the Royal College of Art DBA Inclusive Design Challenge 2005: www.hhrc.rca.ac.uk/events/DBAChallenge/2005/stik.html.

It is named STIK because 'it prods you into action, gets you working, stops you getting stuck and ultimately helps things stick to memory.'

Six areas were identified as causing difficulty at the design brief, generating and presenting ideas stages:

- fixing things to memory

- interpreting content

- focusing on detail

- capturing ideas

- establishing a logical progression

- explaining how ideas are reached in the first place.

The solution centres on these strategies:

- Links are created through storytelling to make language more visual.

- Shapes and colour coding act as memory prompts.

- Repeated sequences and consistent patterns are used.

- Distinctive icons assist memory by association.

- Objects bring intangible actions and ideas to life.

The toolkit has four elements, as discussed below.

STIK 1 – the brief story

Briefs are translated into short stories where background information becomes **the setting**; the client, their product and brand becomes **the hero**; obstacles are **the villain**; deliverables are **the challenge** and the desired result – **the reward**. The client enters briefing information on an A4 colour coordinated pro forma with the five briefing elements as headings. The project leader translates these into the story elements on the reverse of story cards. These contain illustrated symbols to prompt thoughts, make associations and trigger memory.

STIK 2 – the cocoon

Dyslexics excel in generating ideas but have difficulty making sure they do not escape. STIK 2 – a portable, pocket-sized set of illustrated cards called cocoons allows them to sketch down their ideas and brainstorm at any time and anywhere. The illustrations are original, abstract and eye-catching, and designed to allow ideas to be recalled through association with them.

STIK 3 – the home

An organised display unit or 'cocoon bank' of variable size where cocoons can be moved around or discarded.

STIK 4 – thought support map

The magnetic thought support map is a tracking tool that looks forward through the lifetime of a project to each stage of the process. Looking back, it allows the evolution of a concept to be traced for the final presentation. Milestone markers indicate stages of the creative process and there is a 'parking lot' for rested ideas. At each milestone, individual 'thought trackers' record key thoughts on a concept, making it easy to piece together a presentation or story.

Innovative training workshops – Dyslexia and Creativity

An innovative training workshop provided by the Lighthouse in Glasgow (www.thelighthouse.co.uk) is showing that, in an increasingly image-based world, being dyslexic can actually be a positive advantage, particularly for design and technology! It has even been claimed that one of the UK's most successful advertising agencies deliberately employs dyslexics because they think in such a visual, multidimensional way.

'Dyslexia and Creativity' is a one-day session developed by Anne Cunningham who had noticed that a high percentage of staff at the Lighthouse were – like her – dyslexic.

> When people talk about dyslexia, it's usually in terms of failure and not being able to do things. But there is much that I and other dyslexics can do that other people struggle with. For instance, we're often good with 3D and visual and spatial comprehension, and as we are approaching a problem differently dyslexia can help with creative problem solving, which is why people working in teams like having us around. So the 'Dyslexia and Creativity' workshops are about how to get around that learning difficulty that dyslexics have.
>
> (Anne Cunningham, education projects officer, The Lighthouse)

Anne revealed that, at university, she 'found ways around' her dyslexia by actually building models of her essays. 'It was a way of organising my thoughts', she explained 'and once I'd "built" my essay, I could write it.' At primary school, she was so good at interpreting the pictures in her reading books that it was some time before the teacher realised she had a serious problem with words.

On the course the teachers are split up into teams and given a design brief to work on, where they have to solve a problem that requires a visual or 3D outcome, such as making a model of something. It's fun and it's challenging and the best thing is, although many teachers start out not being confident about working in 3D or visually, once they've tried it they start to realise the potential of learning – and teaching – that way.

Tips for the D&T teacher

- Outline what is going to be taught in the lesson, ending the lesson with a résumé of what has been taught. In this way information is more likely to go from short-term memory to long-term memory.

- Consider font size and style, e.g. Comic Sans or Verdana in written work.

- Use diagrams or pictures instead of lengthy written explanations.

- Break tasks down into small easily remembered pieces of information.

- If visual memory is poor, copying must be kept to a minimum. Notes or handouts are far more useful.

- Encourage good organisational skills by the use of folders and dividers to keep work easily accessible and in an orderly fashion.

- When homework is set, it is important to check that the child correctly writes down exactly what is required. Try to ensure that the appropriate worksheets and books are with the child to take home.

Presenting work on an interactive whiteboard/board

- Use different colours for each line if there is a lot of written information.

- Ensure that the writing is well spaced.

Coursework projects in D&T

- Use coloured paper for handouts, or coloured overlays for reading material.

- Use simple, colour-coded systems for filing or organisation.

- Encourage use of spell-checker and thesaurus.

- Consider more advanced software such as text readers or providing audio versions of information.

- Build on and encourage strengths, such as creativity and design and develop coping strategies for weaker areas, e.g. use mind maps for organising.

- Above all, be patient and supportive!

Dyspraxia

Dyspraxia is a label sometimes given to pupils who are in various degrees, clumsy or manifest some inadequacy in controlling material – paper, pencil, tools, etc. Oddly, some of them seem good at hand/eye coordination or can easily catch a ball (while some certainly cannot). It seems possible that dyspraxia is sometimes the result of very swift brain functioning failing to translate into physical action. Thus we get pupils who are very thoughtful and sometimes speedy in their ideas, but who cannot put their thoughts into action.

More specific information can be obtained from the Dyspraxia Foundation, www.dyspraxiafoundation.org.uk.

Here is a description of what it feels like for someone with Dyspraxia to walk through a crowded shopping centre, written by Vicky aged 17.

> Some people don't see crowds as individual people, but as one huge seething mass that sucks them in. They have to physically work out how to bypass people, and they often misjudge distances and bump into things. These people naturally hate being touched. The texture of someone else's clothing brushes their cheek; it's a texture that they can't stand, and they start to feel sick. They think, 'These strangers have no right to invade other people's space – stand back from me!' Fragments of conversation are pulsing through their heads. Everyone else can block out background babble, but these people can't anditsoundsalldistortedandyoustarttopanicsomuch. Cars are zooming by with

huge roaring noises and the floor seems to lurch. The smell of cigarette smoke is thick and irritating and they can't cope. Smells, sights, and sound all jumble together to form a messy porridge that gunges up their brain and they can't THINK.

(Victoria Biggs, *Caged in Chaos: A Dyspraxic Guide to Breaking Free*, 2005)

Imagine what a D&T practical workshop must feel like to this pupil.

'How dyspraxia affects my life'

Matthew describes how dyspraxia affects him at his website

www.matts-hideout.co.uk/dyspraxia/index.php?dyspraxia3.htm.

Dyspraxia effects every part of my life, from when I wake, until I go to sleep. Many able bodied people, can carry out the following simple things with ease and without thinking too hard about it:

- Eating
- Pouring a drink
- Walking through crowds
- Washing and dressing
- Writing
- Running
- Following instructions

I am able bodied. I do not use a wheelchair, I have full use of my arms and legs, in fact I look completely 'normal' (but then, what is normal?) but for me, carrying out the above tasks requires extra concentration and I often do them wrong. For example, while pouring a drink of orange juice, it will miss the cup! I don't know why, but the cup never seems to be where I think it is. Then there is getting dressed, my shoelaces never stay done up! As for socks, how do you get the heal of the sock on your heal? Now using a knife and fork, that's interesting! Cutting food can be a nightmare and spreading butter on toast, well that's always fun. As for following a list of instructions, if I was asked to go upstairs and get a pencil, some paper, a textbook and an eraser, by the time I got upstairs, I would have forgotten what I went up for, and come down just with the pencil!

Anything that requires co-ordination of movement or thought, even a simple thing that many take for granted, causes me difficulties throughout my day. It does become very frustrating, because I know what I want to do but my body sometimes lets me down.

Tips for the D&T teacher

Clothing and overalls for practical work

- Laces, buttons and ties on overalls are difficult – have Velcro fasteners.

- Cut out labels on overalls as they will itch or irritate.

- Allow the pupil to bring their own overall in a material that does not irritate them

Practical work

- Allow the pupil plenty of time to practice essential skills and provide easy-to-handle tools and equipment.

Writing

- Offer different pens to find out which is most comfortable to work with – avoid cartridge pens. Biro, Rollerball, gel pens and pencils will be best.

- Allow working on a computer as much as possible as the pupil will get thoughts down quicker and complete work faster.

- When doing charts, lists and calculations, the pupil may not be able to line up the columns very well. Encourage the use of squared paper and they find it easier to line up the columns.

Organisation

- Have organised places for everything in the room and on the desks or work areas, e.g. use pencil pots and plastic containers of different sizes, labelled.

- Make lists of things to remember and attach them to the folder.

- Post-it notes are useful as well. Encourage the pupil to use them to mark pages in books and write notes to remember things.

- Give instructions slowly and give one instruction at a time. Be patient if they have to ask you to repeat it, or to write it down.

- Have a project or D&T noticeboard, where they can check what is going on. Have a calendar and an organiser for project work.

Confidence and self-esteem

- Centre projects around the interests of the pupil.

- Encourage the pupil to be individualistic and innovative in their design ideas. Explain that it is hard to make a mistake in design ideas as it's all about experimentation and interpretation. Encourage the pupils to express themselves through what they design and make.

Senses

- Food technology teachers need to be aware that some pupils with dyspraxia will find the feel of some foods in their mouth unbearable. Allow the pupil to choose the products that they are going to taste during product evaluation, and allow them to opt out of the tasting part.

- Try to keep the noise levels to a minimum, and position a pupil away from machinery to prevent sensory overload

Attitudes towards these gifted pupils

It might be that all Asperger syndrome pupils are 'gifted' and many ADHD pupils seem so. Giftedness is often combined with dyspraxia and there are some experts who think all dyslexic pupils tend towards high ability. But the fact that behavioural difficulties are so often associated with these categories of pupils reinforces the way teachers, parents and pupils themselves may react to the situation.

It may be that all these categories have a positive prognosis, but they are all predominantly seen in a negative light, and this will quickly transmit from parents and professionals to the pupils themselves. This will tend to undermine their self-confidence.

Curricular needs

> I gained the lowest pass grades in my 5 GCSEs in my school, and I was so ashamed of my performance until my wonderful Scottish history teacher took me to one side and said that given my difficulties at home she was prouder of me than any other child in my school – those few words lit my darkness.
>
> (Claire Curtis-Thomas MP)

Although each of these groups has a unique condition, all those pupils require an environment that will develop their gifts, provision to address their learning disability and emotional support to deal with their inconsistent abilities. Four general guidelines can help to meet the needs of these pupils.

1. Nurture their gift

In the past we have focused on addressing the learning difficulties first, but it is important not to focus on the weaknesses as this results in poor self-esteem, a lack of motivation, depression and stress. Develop their strengths, interests and superior intellectual capacities with a stimulating classroom environment and enrichment activities designed to minimise weaknesses and to highlight creative thinking and innovation.

2. Provide a nurturing environment that values individual differences

Success in the real world depends on skills or knowledge in other areas besides reading and writing. D&T provides an opportunity for pupils to contribute and feel valued, and to understand their own needs and wants better. A nurturing D&T classroom is one that develops individual pupils' potential – values and respects individual differences. Pupils are offered a number of different ways of approaching a design brief, according to their learning style. They can respond to researching and presenting in a way that works for them. Remember, these pupils do not want the curriculum to be less challenging or demanding. Rather, they need alternative ways to work. They are encouraged to work collaboratively in teams and support each other. Pupils are rewarded for what they do well.

3. Encourage compensation strategies

The following list outlines suggestions for providing compensation techniques to assist the pupil:

- Find sources of information that are appropriate for pupils who may have difficulty reading. Some examples are videos, visual websites, games, visits, interviews, photographs and practical work.

- Provide organisers to help pupils receive and communicate information. Teach pupils who have difficulty transferring ideas to a sequential format on paper to use brainstorming and webbing to generate outlines and organise written work. Provide management plans in which tasks are listed sequentially with target dates for completion. Finally, provide a structure or visual format to guide the finished product. A sketch of portfolio contents pages will enable these pupils to produce a well-organised product.

- Use ICT to promote productivity. It is efficient to organise and access information, increase accuracy and enhance the visual quality of the finished product. It allows pupils with learning disabilities to hand in work of which they can feel proud.

- Offer a variety of options for communication of ideas, not just written – recorded, digital photo stories, annotated sketchbooks, comic strip, etc.

- Help pupils who have problems in short-term memory develop strategies for remembering. The use of mnemonics, especially those created by pupils themselves, is one effective strategy to enhance memory.

4. Encourage awareness of individual strengths and weaknesses

These pupils need to understand their abilities, strengths and weaknesses, so that they can make intelligent choices about their future. Mentoring by adults (for example existing designers) who are gifted and learning-disabled will help them believe that such individuals can succeed.

INSET activity – Who are the most able pupils and what strategies can be used to identify them?

This activity looks at the four case studies (on CD) of pupils who are most able. Some are gifted and talented and others are gifted, but with other special needs. The objectives of this activity are:

1. to broaden their view of 'most able' that they might teach

2. to share strategies for planning and managing work in D&T lessons to meet very specific needs

3. to plan a project taking into account how it can be adapted for the individual pupil.

What you will need

- A set of case studies copied from the CD, with sufficient copies for staff to discuss and comment on in twos or threes. You can use the case studies provided, or perhaps add to these ones from your own school and department.

- Strategy card packs – there is a template on the CD that you can use to make these cards, as shown opposite.

What to do

1. Give each two or three teachers a case study to share and ask them to read the commentary about the pupil (2 minutes).

2. Ask them to discuss what strengths this pupil will have in D&T and the strategies that can be used in the classroom. Ask them to add to the list of bullets provided (8–10 minutes).

3. Think of a project that they currently use with this year group and how they can adapt it for this pupil's needs. Ask them to write a summary of the design brief, focused practical tasks and product evaluation activities, etc. that the pupil will engage in (15–20 minutes).

4. Bring the group together and discuss the case studies in turn, adding to the bullets lists with further suggestions and ideas for planning and managing projects.

5. Add these completed examples and any other that is relevant to your school or most able cohort to your departmental handbook.

STRATEGY CARDS	Encourage pupils to respect the opinions and ideas of others and express their own opinions, e.g. review the questions you ask pupils to use during researching and evaluation activities.
Encourage socialising with their peers – organise paired and group work regularly.	Encourage pupils to reflect on their own learning and think about how they make progress, e.g. add reflection time and activities during project.
Use learning mentors – older pupil or someone from outside school.	Listen to pupils' views on how they like to learn and provide opportunities for this, but encourage pupils to develop other learning strategies also.
Visits to designers, manufacturers, engineering plants, and work-based learning.	Use wrong answers as a learning opportunity.
Give pupils opportunities to consider questions/problems to which there is no definitive answer.	Provide higher level tasks than usual in lessons; provide a bank of higher level extension activities to encourage all pupils to aspire to a high standard.
Provide individually negotiated design and make assignments.	Provide differentiated assessment criteria.
Use displays or case studies of aspirational work to raise expectations	Allow pupils to present their project work in a variety of different ways, for example portfolio, e-portfolio, presentation in assembly, story-telling
Encourage the use of ICT to extend work – extend information available, resources, tools and software.	Share customs, rules and traditions for the way designers and engineers work, to explain processes and methods.
Monitor the time pupils spend waiting for others to catch up and plan work for pupils that is highly motivating.	Allow pupils to concentrate on projects and topics that capture their interest.
Position pupils so that they are not distracted or overcome by noisy equipment.	Organise the practical room so that pupils can access equipment and resources as independently as possible.
Set pupils in year groups.	Clubs, e.g. Young Engineers Club.

CHAPTER 5

Classroom provision

> I owe my present career to one dedicated teacher who believed in my abilities and nurtured my potential through building my communication skills, both visual and aural. He gave me the greatest foundation in using communication to convey complex things clearly and succinctly.
>
> (Paul Turnock, Brunel University School of Engineering and Design, www.brunel.ac.uk/about/acad/sed)

What do you do when a Year 7 pupil arrives who already performs at Level 8? What do you aim for next? How can you provide for their needs?

Three things are essential for the learning environment of these pupils:

- projects that encourage each pupil to develop their individual potential with access to other designer-makers of similar ability

- teaching values that enhance their D&T capability, talent, creativity and decision-making

- opportunities to develop and use higher levels of thinking, such as analysis, synthesis and evaluation.

Many of the approaches described in this chapter are about effective differentiation; these benefit all learners, not just the most able.

High expectations

> I would advise any young aspiring designer to absorb knowledge left, right and centre. Visit design fairs and exhibitions, read design books and magazines avidly, arrange to do work experience with a variety of design firms and talk to as many designers as possible. I would also suggest they spend time learning a craft or several crafts as understanding how things

are actually made and how different materials shape the design process is fundamental to good design practice.

(Sir Terence Conran, restaurateur, furniture designer and entrepreneur)

It is important that teachers have high expectations of gifted and talented pupils and that classroom activities provide opportunities for pupils to express and develop their special abilities. Activities that encourage all pupils to think creatively, explore and develop ideas, and try different approaches will help to minimise the social pressures to conform that might apply to very able pupils. All pupils will benefit from the creative and investigative approaches and problem solving activities in design and technology. Opportunities to make comparisons and to provide evaluative and critical comments are particularly important. Gifted and talented pupils should have opportunities to set their own questions, offer opinions and views, explanations and justifications, to interpret information and reflect on design and technological issues.

Working beyond the level of their peers

Teachers need to develop teaching and learning programmes for design and technology that ensure that each pupil reaches as high a standard as possible and that gifted and talented pupils are working at a level that will allow them to develop knowledge and skills beyond those that are expected of the rest of their class or year. They will need to ensure that the provision that is made caters for pupils with different learning styles and different talents. Teachers will need to set higher targets for gifted and talented pupils and respond to their needs by offering them opportunities to pursue topics in greater depth or at a greater level of challenge, to tackle a wider range of tasks, or to work through activities at a faster pace. The engagement of able pupils with the planned work of the class may require special management. For example: it can be helpful to give them opportunities to work with other able pupils; to allow them to take special roles in mixed ability groups; to provide opportunities for them to work with older pupils who are enthusiasts; or to receive support from an able older person. There is a need to monitor the progress of pupils and review targets regularly to ensure that the provision that is made is effective in enhancing performance in design and technology. As with the identification of gifted and talented pupils, procedures for assessing progress will involve a range of factors including performance in assessment tests or tasks, approaches to tackling problems and investigations, and responses to questions.

Effective differentiation

Pupils can be encouraged to use their talents in ways that they find exciting and interesting by providing differentiated tasks with extension work or seeking opportunities for enrichment work within or outside of design and technology lessons. When preparing extension or enrichment work, while the nature of the task might be open-ended, teachers need to be clear about the processes involved and the outcomes that are expected. Activities should have clear goals and aim to increase ability to analyse and solve problems, and stimulate originality, initiative and self-direction.

Care needs to be taken if providing additional work for gifted and talented pupils to avoid this being viewed by them as an imposition and reducing their motivation. It is also important to ensure that there is a careful balance between the provision of special opportunities for individuals or groups of pupils and their inclusion in the mainstream academic and social life of the class. It is not desirable to create an elite group within a class or year, which results in pupils with less ability feeling that they are of less importance or that their achievements are not valued. Teachers also need to ensure that the most able pupils are not expected to work unsupported and undirected for extended periods.

Guidance on using the activities within the Key Stage 3 Strategy D&T programme to provide challenge, motivate and engage and support independent learning for able pupils can be found on the CD that accompanies this book (Key Stage 3 Strategy and Most Able PDF).

A useful resources list can also be found on the CD – books and websites are included.

Planning and managing units of work

To our core or standard D&T scheme of work we are looking to add depth, breadth and pace.

What are we aiming to develop?

- depth in pupils' knowledge, skills and understanding

- thinking like a designer/technologist

- intellectual playfulness – risk-taking and rule breaking

- self-regulation and self-direction

- discussion, debate and argument around key D&T ideas

- exposure to others with high levels of expertise in D&T.

Depth, breadth and pace can be planned into the three activities that makeup D&T – design and make assignments (DMAs), focused practical tasks and product evaluation activities.

Planning demanding DMAs for your most able pupils

Teachers will need to negotiate individual designing and making assignments for more able pupils. Specific extra demands can be built into design briefs and higher expectations set. Pupils should be allowed greater freedom to choose or greater control over their projects and design briefs – projects they have chosen, more challenging projects than the rest of the class, projects that link with outside companies and experts, projects that take them to issues and contexts that are unfamiliar and are more demanding in their solution.

It is important for design and make assignments (DMA) to be pupil directed. Without the pupil having ownership, the DMA becomes merely an activity or exercise. The teacher's role is about allowing the pupil to take the lead and then choosing when to intervene, for example to suggest redirection for the pupil or to negotiate more demanding work with them.

Intervention can happen informally in classroom conversations or can be formal through tutorials.

INSET activity

What to do

Review your current designing and making assignments or design briefs that you set the class.

Questions

- Identify which DMAs provide appropriate opportunities for more demanding criteria to be used with some pupils?

- Discuss with your teaching team what additional criteria could be added or what changes could be made.

- Discuss how this will be presented to the class and the individuals.

There is a checklist to review your current DMA projects on the CD.

I believe there is real value in having a broad understanding of what Design is and how it affects our lives, regardless of a pupil wishing to pursue a career in the D&T fields. Communication and problem solving are key to most industries – this is why Design and Technology should be as highly regarded as other core subjects.

(Donna Fullman, Design Director of Eyefood, www.eyefood.net)

Case study 1 – Renegotiating the design brief with an able pupil

Year 9 Corporate Identity

This project is adapted from the original SCAA optional task and test for Year 9, and the QCA/DfES scheme of work Unit 9C 'Using ICT To Link with the World Outside School'.

Design and make assignment – Corporate Identity

Souvenirs and collectables, e.g. T shirts, 3D signs and models are used to promote events, pop stars, cartoon characters and even schools. Design and make a coordinated range of promotional products for a special occasion or a client.

Pupils usually spend Key Stage 3 working on a series of projects focused on a specific material such as food, textiles or resistant materials. This unit provides a Design and Make Assignment where pupils work across materials areas and draw on their understanding and skills from all parts of D&T. Pupils work as a team to design and make a coordinated range of promotional products, e.g. for a local event or a commercial company. One aim of this unit is to give pupils an opportunity to use ICT to work collaboratively on a design and make project. ICT has transformed the way that pupils can work in teams and gain access to expertise outside the classroom by using e-mail, conferencing and electronic whiteboards. Team projects can be undertaken with other schools, and shared design software means that pupils can work on projects together. They use ICT effectively to help them work collaboratively on the project, drawing on expertise and help from outside the school, and using CAD/CAM (computer-aided design and manufacture).

Another aim of this project is to highlight the range of generic designing strategies they have learned when working with diverse materials and how they can apply those generic skills to their chosen examination area at Key Stage 4.

Provision for more able pupils

A teacher negotiated this DMA with a pupil so that the pupil:

- worked with a company outside the school who identified a challenging design specification and required that the products were innovative, but also thoroughly tested and of marketable quality

- designed for an event that was not familiar and required rigorous research

- negotiated their work directly with the company, working independently as far as possible

- was ambitious in the range of products they chose and ideas they presented and thus took greater risks and coped with a greater number of variables

- drew on a range of experiences across the different materials areas and applied them during the project

- provided a business plan for the company demonstrating the production costs of the range and suggested selling prices

- made a presentation to the company showing their prototypes and business plan.

Objectives

Designing:

- combine ideas from a variety of sources

- be prepared to take risks when generating ideas through a range of creative and critical thinking techniques

- adopt an appropriate role within a group.

Making:

- draft a plan for batch production that will enable them to produce their chosen idea

- suggest alternative ways of working to overcome any problems

- demonstrate a skilful use of a wide range of techniques during trialling and production, including: measuring, marking out, cutting and joining; decorative and construction techniques; quality checking

- devise tests and evaluate the effectiveness. Suggest improvements to their design.

Managing the project

It is important that the department plans as a team so that pupils are able to draw on knowledge, skills and understanding from across the materials areas and previous projects to reinforce their learning. The intention is that pupils work as a team to explore and generate design ideas, developing themes and images for a product range – manufactured in a range of materials, such as food, metal, plastics, wood and textiles.

This is also used as a test to inform pupils and teachers about levels of achievement.

Resources

- QCA/DfES Unit 9C, 'Using ICT to link with the world outside school', www.standards.dfes.gov.uk/schemes2/secondary_dt/dat09c

- DfES Key Stage 3 National Strategy Foundation Subjects: D&T programme (module 4 Designing)

- Bright Ideas CD, www.data.org.uk.

Structure of the project

Investigating the context (Lessons 1–4)

The teacher introduces the design brief and organises the pupils into teams. In small groups the pupils discuss the task and the issues that the task addresses such as:

- what the product will need to be like if it is to be attractive to potential customers

- the main features of a successful product

- appropriate materials and techniques for multiple production.

Evaluating existing products

In small groups the pupils:

- analyse the products in terms of form, function, appearance, novelty appeal

- analyse the materials, components and construction

- compare products and identify strengths and weaknesses.

The teacher shows the pupils how to use two evaluating strategies – ACCESS FM and Compare and Contrast (from Module 4 of the national training for D&T) (see CD for more information about these activities).

Exploring and handling a collection of possible materials and stimulus for ideas

The pupils examine a range of materials, with different characteristics and properties, and aesthetic qualities and using a variety of manufacturing and finishing processes, including some that are unusual applications and interpretations. Pupils use the materials to model some ideas and for sketching and note making.

The pupils evaluate the success of their modelled ideas as products designed to meet specific requirements.

In a combination of individual and group work, the pupils improve an existing product or idea developed in earlier activities. Development involves generating, modelling and testing ideas in a range of materials, and producing sample products.

They agree as a team on the design theme for their product range and ways that it can be outputted to a range of different materials using CAD/CAM. Each pupil should end up with a design for making. Pupils plan how they are going to make the products in the group.

Lessons 5–7

The products are made and tested using the pupils' plans.

Lesson 8

Pupils give short presentations as a team with an evaluation of the project and then take an individual test.

Pupil test

1. Make a sketch of your design for the product range. Label to show what each part of the product range was made from and how it was constructed.

2. Choose one part of your product range that could be better designed. State why and how it could be improved.

3. Explain the link between your product and the event, attraction or service for which it was produced.

4. Describe two techniques that are used to make one product in your range, interesting to look at.

5. Describe two finishing techniques you considered for one product in your range. List the tools and equipment needed for each finish and say what each tool would be used for.

6. Draw a flow diagram to show the main stages for batch production for one product in your range.

7. Describe two quality checks you carried out and why they were needed.

8. Describe the user testing that you did.

Some additional questions for more able pupils could be:

1. Why have these particular materials been chosen?

2. How would you test this to see . . .?

3. Propose an alternative solution to the product or part of product.

4. How else would you . . .?

5. Suggest changes you could make to . . .

6. What effect will this product have on people's lives and relationships?

7. What could be done better or differently?

Case study 2 – Allowing the pupil to choose their own project

Year 9 Our Own Class project

It is common in Key Stage 4 and post-16 for pupils to choose their own project. An able pupil should have the opportunity to do this earlier with support from the teacher and the class.

This project is built upon two units from the QCA/DfES Scheme of work Unit 9F 'Moving onto Key Stage 4' and Unit 9B 'Designing for Markets'.

Inclusive designing

A small manufacturing company has asked you to design and make a prototype of a product for use at home that will appeal to older people. The company wants to achieve the 'Owl Mark' for this product, and wants you to think about the following statement in your design of the product: 'Design for the young and you exclude the old. Design for the old and you include the young'. This reinforces the fact that you, as a designer, will need to have empathy with those who will use your designs.

This is an opportunity for the pupils to work on a class project together, where they negotiate and agree a task that they would all like to work on. It can link to a current or topical issue, for example raising money for a charity or as part of a local or national event that coincides with the school project.

The design solution can just be taken to a proposal stage, where groups are asked to present their idea and how they would go about it. But most of all it is important to review what makes a good choice of a project and to rehearse this with pupils who are about to choose their own projects in Key Stage 4.

This design brief was presented by the teacher as a possibility, which was then renegotiated with the class.

Provision for more able pupils

Design briefs can seem very artificial to pupils. They can seem as if they come from nowhere, whereas for designing to be done well, it relies on pupils' understanding what they are doing and why. More able pupils should be able to identify their own tasks for projects and during Key Stage 3 we must prepare them for this by revealing the purposes of an assignment, both in terms of designing purposes and learning purposes.

One of the main areas for progression is that of moving from the pupils receiving a design brief from the teacher, to a situation where they are choosing and negotiating tasks with the teacher.

One further area of progression is to ask pupils to design for the needs of others, and to explore unfamiliar circumstances.

Objectives

Design and make assignment:

- to carry out a design and make assignment in negotiation with the teacher, and prepare and follow a design brief

- to design and make a product, by bringing together what they have learnt during the key stage, and by applying the knowledge, skills and understanding they developed during the product evaluation activities and focused practical tasks.

Product evaluation and focused practical tasks:

- how to assess people's needs, for example select and use appropriate techniques to help them understand the situation in which a product is used, e.g. carry out an observational study or interview

- how case studies or observation can be used to clarify people's needs and wants

- how to generate criteria to evaluate products that are designed to meet users' needs, about the effect that a client's lifestyle and personal situation can have on designing, and how a user interacts with their environment

- suggest improvements to designs of products so that they are more appropriate for older people, and justify their suggestions in terms of values (their own and those they have learnt to respect in others). This may involve discussion of some of the ethical issues that result from the conflicting demands faced by designers.

Resources

- QCA/DfES Unit 9F, 'Moving onto KS4: reviewing and target-setting' and Unit 9B, 'Designing for markets – mini enterprise': www.standards.dfes. gov.uk/schemes2/secondary_dt/

- DfES Key Stage 3 National Strategy Foundation Subjects: D&T programme (module 4 Designing) Activities: Role Play and user needs, Live like the user, Observe people and products

- www.designcouncil.info/inclusivedesignresource

- Helen Hamlyn Research at the Royal College of Art: www.hhrc.rca.ac.uk

- Designing to make a difference: www.lemelson.org/utility/latdc_movie.php (Quicktime video on inclusive design)

- Inclusive design: ESL Industries, www.eslindustries.com: special needs products.

Structure of the project

Lesson 1

The teacher introduces the project by showing a short video on inclusive design, 'Designing to make a difference', and in small groups the pupils discuss a list of headlines.

Pupil sheet – Headlines

'Design for the young and you exclude the old. Design for the old and you include the young'.

There are already 130 million people over 50 in the European Union. By 2020, one in every two European adults will be over that age.

'Dependable' networked 'smart' or assistive home technology systems should enable the person to retain a quality of life and independence within their own home.

By 2020 every second European adult – all 130 million of us – will be over 50.

In the West, growing evidence suggests that the effect of improved diet, medicine and living conditions is to prolong not just life expectancy but active life.

One in every three British adults is already over 50.

The over 50s in the UK already hold more than 60% of all savings.

Taking early retirement and looking forward to an increasingly active 'third age' of healthy, independent life after work, these people will make demands for new products and services.

For the past 40+ years industry and commerce have aimed products at young people, ignoring the needs of older people.

From packaging to fashion, design can create unnecessary obstacles to older people.

Design with older people in mind will be multi-generational, inclusive, universal and in every sense better design – it will certainly not be boring.

The teacher asks the class to spend time with an elderly relative or neighbour, observe them carrying out everyday tasks, and report back in two weeks, describing any difficulties they noticed. The teacher emphasises that it's not solutions that they are after at this stage – just the problems.

Module 4 from the Key Stage 3 Foundation Subjects D&T national programme provides some useful supporting activities for the introduction, such as role-play and user needs, live like the user, observe people and products.

Lessons 2–5

The teacher asks each pupil to talk about their observations, and records the problems as a list on a flipchart.

The teacher then discusses with the class which design challenges might realistically be tackled in the time allowed for the project. They discuss and vote for the problems they would like to address.

The class divides into groups to tackle four problems:

- hanging out the washing

- picking up dog mess

- carving a joint of meat

- picking items up from the floor.

The groups brainstorm possible solutions and develop some of their ideas. They make prototypes as they design.

Lesson 6

Each group presents their final idea using a range of methods including slide shows, exhibitions and video.

Part of this example draws on a project at Launceston College, which worked with Kenneth Grange, product designer from Pentagram, and facilitated by the Design Council.

Planning extension and enrichment activities – focused practical tasks and product evaluation

The teacher's aim is to extend the work for some and to enhance the work for others. Extension tasks expect pupils to do more parts of a project, carrying out activities that others do not. Enrichment refers to some pupils doing the same activities as others, but carrying these out more thoroughly or at a more sophisticated level.

Extension and enrichment activities require it to be accepted as normal by the class that different members of the group work to different targets.

Extending focused practical tasks

Teachers can plan optional extension activities, such as additional focused practical tasks to expect more of the most able pupils.

Focused practical tasks are led by the teachers and are used to teach the knowledge, skills and understanding that pupils need for the DMA. Some tasks are essential for all pupils to do. Others can be used as additional extension activities. These can be completed during class work or homework These optional activities can be used with gifted and talented pupils to develop an extended range of designing and making skills and a wider range of techniques and ideas for them to draw on during the DMA, and consequently approach the DMA in a more demanding way.

Questions for an INSET activity

Review your current scheme of work:

- What are the essential activities for all pupils?

- What extension activities could be provided for gifted and talented pupils?

- How will you organise and manage the extension activities?

Case study 3 – Year 8 Textiles: Juggling Balls

Design and make a juggling kit for a celebration, consisting of a themed bag/ container and matching juggling shapes. All the juggling shapes should be identical, so you will need to consider production aids to help you batch-produce identical shapes (www.standards.dfes.gov.uk/schemes2/secondary_dt/dato8eiii).

The teacher used the scheme of work unit to identify essential activities that the whole class took part in and two further optional activities that only some of the pupils did. In the original QCA unit these focused on manufacturing.

Two essential activities

- In order to review progress, revise techniques that pupils are familiar with from Year 7, and introduce a range of manufacturing techniques needed for the DMA. Pupils should revise health and safety regulations and, where appropriate, should test and compare different tools and pieces of equipment for the same task. Pupils could practise their skills by making a simple item from a design or plan they are given.
- Show pupils examples of how manufacturing aids can be made or used to help with volume production. Discuss with them how they should take into account the use of manufacturing aids when making. Discuss how designing and making identical parts in a batch, using CAD/CAM or other manufacturing aids, can be cost-effective and ensure accuracy.

Two optional activities

- Discuss with the pupils how identical parts can be made using CAD/CAM or other manufacturing aids.
- Revise or demonstrate to the pupils how to use CAD/CAM for making single items and for small batch production, and discuss when it is appropriate to use ICT. Discuss with the pupils the use of a computer-controlled machine to realise their design, including safety points and technical advice. Allow the pupils to practise their skills by making a simple product, identified by the teacher. Make sure that the pupils have an opportunity to practise the skills they will need during the DMA.

The teachers also added further extension activities for the designing part of the project, to extend the more able pupils' strategies to come up with innovative design ideas. The teachers planned these carefully so that the pupils enjoyed and were challenged by the 'extra' tasks. They were chosen as they were very relevant to the project and fitted in well with the other class activities at the time.

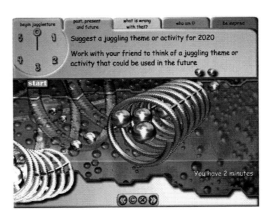

Making extra researching fun

To support generating and developing ideas, a set of interesting and trusted web links were offered to the pupils which gave them extra structured research, games and activities to do. The teacher chose links to information about juggling that the pupil may not have thought about to engage them in wider debates about their design ideas and the context they are working in. These were presented in a multimedia file, such as PowerPoint, and the pupils were able to choose which links they wanted to spend some time on. For example, looking to the future – what would juggling themes and activities look like in 2020? (see further information on the CD to support 'future' activities, e.g. Get Out of Your Box, New From Old, In 10 years' time).

> Open your mind to the possibilities of future technologies, future materials technologies and, most importantly, begin to develop a true empathy for people and their particular needs when designing new products to suit their own lifestyles and to operate within their own context. Everything is redesignable given these three key cornerstones of change.
>
> (Paul Turnock, Brunel University School of Engineering and Design, www.brunel.ac.uk/about/acad/sed)

For example, use web links to find out about the history and traditions of juggling with some interesting case studies.

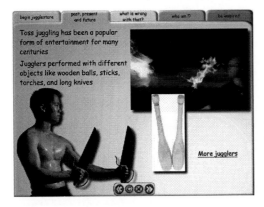

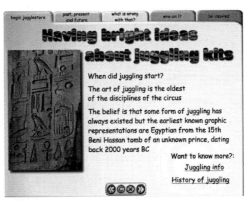

Juggling (all similar images in this chapter are from LT Davies, *Year 7 Bright Ideas*, Design and Technology Association; all photographs © 2006 Jupiterimages Corporation)

Random word linking

The teacher gave the pupils a series of pictures and asked them to come up with words to describe how the picture looks as well as how it feels.

For example, the teacher used a picture of a reptile and came up with the words, such as *cold, slimy, scary, scales, leathery, creepy, ugly*.

The pupils were then asked to link these ideas to possible themes for their juggling kits.

The pictures used were of penguins, a feather, an apple orchard, a futurist building, an iceberg, and so on. It encourages the pupils to think freely and creatively, putting to one side their preconceptions about what a juggling kit theme should be. The teacher showed word associations being done quickly, with humour and unusual associations, without analysing words. They asked pupils to use this strategy when they are generating ideas or when they are

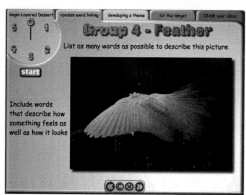

Random word linking

stuck. It was an interesting homework to set and pupils could also try online word association at:

- Google Sets (labs.google.com/sets)
- One Look (www.onelook.com).

See further information on the accompanying CD (Word Association, Be Wacky).

'What if' questions

At a point in the project, particularly if the teacher thought that an able pupil was coasting, she used the 'What if' activity to add a new challenge or dimension to the pupils thinking. These questions can be changed according to the design brief. They encourage higher order thinking.

What if . . . the fabric you have chosen to use . . . is now heavily taxed because of environmental reasons?	What if . . . no packaging was allowed for this product, except that which was part of the design?
What if . . . this product was now banned for children?	What if . . . the same design idea as yours is produced by a competitor next week?
What if . . . you had to design it for disabled as well as able bodied?	What if . . . you had to be able to use it in the outdoors as well as indoors?
What if . . . you had to be able to flat-pack it for transport and storage?	What if . . . you had to make this for half the cost?

What if cards

Enrichment activities for the most able

> She taught me to organise my thoughts, to do research, to talk and listen, to seek alternatives, to resolve old problems with new solutions, to argue logically. Above all, she taught me not to believe in anything blindly, to doubt, and to question, even that which seems to be irrefutably true . . .
>
> (Isabel Allende 2001)

Teachers can adapt focused practical tasks and product evaluation activities so that there is a difference in pace and demand.

In product evaluation tasks, depth can be added to the activities by asking pupils to explore values issues and encouraging critical thinking, for example:

- the benefit and disadvantages to the users of products and others
- consider the impact of the product on a wider range of people
- evaluation of environmental impact, of unintended outcomes
- balance social issues with financial ones when evaluating their own and others' designs.

Questions for an INSET activity

Take a product evaluation activity

- Ask yourself, 'What is the normal level of result you realistically expect for this activity?'

- Then identify what a much better than normal result might look like

- How will you identify those who might need to work differently from the norm?

- How will the work be varied to accommodate them?

- Identify where you may need to catch a pupil early in an activity and talk them through, for example better quality research, using a wider range of source material, a larger number of initial ideas and/or more detailed testing.

Case study 4 – Year 9 Smart and Modern Materials

The teacher at Hassenbrook School in Essex was working with the QCA Unit 9A(i) 'Selecting Materials', where there are some product evaluation activities about smart and modern materials.

- Ask the pupils to explore how the development of new materials/ingredients and technologies has allowed designers to achieve things that were not possible before, e.g. we can now make materials/ingredients with the properties that we want, and in the future we are likely to see materials made to measure for a huge range of applications.
- Ask the pupils to consider the wider implication of choosing a particular way of meeting a need or solving a problem. They could think about whether meeting the need is worth the resources required and whether the proposed solution has other consequences that should be taken into account (e.g. concerns about biodiversity, GM crops, the use of growth hormones and antibiotics in the production of food).

Different pupils could approach this same activity in a number of ways. This activity was extended for very able pupils. Selected Year 9 pupils took part in an online debate on genetically modified foods. The debate, organised by Anglia Campus, enabled pupils to put questions to Professor Peter Bromley of the Royal Holloway College and Dr Douglas Barr of Greenpeace. Pupils worked independently and were allowed one hour to research genetically modified foods and to prepare questions. The use of the internet to interactively access remote sources in this way was shown to be a positive approach for working with able pupils.

Case study 5 – Year 7 Sport Accessories and Kits

The textiles teacher was working with the Year 7 QCA Unit 7A(iii) 'Understanding Materials'. There is a suggested product evaluation activity:

> ● Ask the pupils to examine a range of existing products, for example pupils could investigate in small groups a selection of sports kit for different functions, which have a range of features

And a suggested extension task:

> ● Some pupils may also be able to consider the impact of a product beyond the purpose for which it was designed.

All pupils in this lesson were examining sports kits. The teacher organised differentiation in the groups by prearranging the groups according to ability and matching the range of products and questions given to their abilities. The more able pupils were asked to look at a more complex range of items, with advanced features and manufacturing processes. She also asked them to consider the impact of the sports accessories beyond the purpose for which they were designed. For example, she added questions to their worksheets that asked them about the crossover of sports kit into fashion products, the cost/profit of products, sponsorship featured on sports kit, new materials and the recycling of fabrics.

Case study 6 – Year 9 Special Diets

The teacher was working with the class on the QCA Unit 9A(i) 'Food: Specialist Diets'. The pupils are asked to design and make a meal for people with special dietary needs.

Next they evaluate a variety of existing ready-made meals for special diets or particular nutritional needs. They are asked to consider how the designers have tried to meet users' needs and preferences, and what constraints there would have been. They investigate how they could adapt these existing ideas and improve each meal's nutritional content for a particular dietary requirement.

The main learning objectives for this activity are:

● how to design food products to meet specific nutritional requirements, and *be able to suggest how to adapt ready prepared meals to change their nutritional content, such as reducing the fat or sugar content*

● how to use hedonic ranking on a five-point scale and difference tests, e.g. paired comparison tests, triangle test and *be able to evaluate food products using these techniques.*

The teacher focuses on using effective questioning techniques and activities to deliver these objectives. The teacher plans which questions to ask, but also plans to stage or sequence those questions so that they guide the pupils towards key lesson objectives.

The teacher also plans higher order questions to stretch the most able. A detailed lesson plan is provided on the accompanying CD.

INSET activity – planning product evaluation questions

Review the product evaluation questions that you use. Are they mainly from the start of the list in the table opposite? Do you ask questions that are at the end of the list? Can you set different questions for groups in the class and match them to their ability?

Adding pace in lessons for more able pupils

More able pupils benefit from fast moving activities, with clearly planned episodes of learning. A degree of autonomy within tasks and opportunity to manage their own time within lessons also allow them some independence from teacher direction.

Case study 7 – Year 8 Wallets

Year 8 pupils are designing and making a wallet for a particular purpose. They develop a standard prototype that can be varied or personalised for particular clients. The teacher plans objectives for the majority of the class, and then supplements these with additional objectives for the more able. The teacher then matches the activities for the lesson to these objectives, and sequences them to ensure pace and engagement.

This lesson is one of a series during the designing part of the project and the main objectives for the lesson are for pupils to:

1. **generate ideas**

   - use a range of materials to stimulate the imagination and use a range of sources of information mainly provided by the teacher

   - In addition more able pupils will combine ideas from a variety of sources, record and share ideas with others, gather and use constructive feedback to develop a proposal.

2. **develop and model ideas**

   - explore, experiment and respond intuitively to allow ideas to develop

   - model ideas to try them out, explore, experiment and select appropriate materials

   - in addition, more able pupils will develop different strategies to elaborate, embellish, expand and develop design ideas, seek opinions of potential users of the product.

3. **plan**

   - work independently on short tasks and manage time within a lesson.

The teacher's lesson plan is provided on the accompanying CD.

Planning product evaluation questions

Knowledge – factual, recall and recognition
- Describe the product
- What is it made from?
- Who is it for?
- When would it be used?
- Where is it used?
- How often is it used?
- Which one . . .
- What is the best one for doing . . .?
- How much does it cost?
- Where is it sold?
- Who designed and made this?
- How has it been made?
- Where is it from?
- What sort/type/category of product is it?
- What other products are like this?

Comprehension – translating, interpreting and extrapolating
- Do I like it?
- Is it what I need?
- Is it the right size, shape, pattern, colour, smell, taste?
- Is it safe?
- Does it do the intended job?
- Is it value for money?
- What is its cost in relation to the income of the potential users?
- Demonstrate how the product is used
- Explain why this product was developed
- Explain what is meant by . . . (label or product feature)
- Give an example of
- Is this the same as . . .?
- What would happen if this product was used for . . . (another purpose)

Application – to situations that are new, new slants
- What is my reaction to this product?
- Who might the owner be?
- Why might they want to buy it?
- Does it work well?
- What ingredients and processes have been used? Why?
- Does it do what it was intended to?
- Does it look and taste good?
- How well is it made?
- Is it nicely finished?
- Is the cost appropriate?
- Is it really needed?
- How much will this product change people's lives?
- Choose the best statements that apply to this product (statements given)
- How is it promoted and packaged?
- Predict what would happen if . . .

Analysis – breaking down into parts, forms
- What is the function of this product/part of the product?
- What do people think of this product?
- Does everyone think this product is a good invention?
- Who is it for?
- What assumptions have been made about the people who might use it?
- Whose needs or wants were possibly considered during designing and making this product?
- Why is this product like this?
- What are the motives of the people who design and make it?
- What is the relationship between this product and . . .?
- What makes this product distinct from others of its type?
- Does this product have an identity or image?
- How has this been achieved?
- Does the promotion target a particular age group or group of people?
- What are they trying to say about the product?
- How are they persuading you?
- What do people believe about this product – is it true?

Synthesis – combining elements into a pattern not clearly there before
- Would I want to own or use it?
- What would this reveal about me?
- What influenced the appearance and the way it works?
- How might the design have been developed?
- How would you test this to see . . .?
- Propose an alternative solution to the product or part of product?
- How else would you . . .?
- Suggest changes you could make to . . .
- Develop a list of important features . . .
- How is this product different from one from 5 years ago/another culture?
- How will this product be different in 10 years time?
- What would happen if you were to add . . .?
- What would happen if you were to make it?
- Why did the designer make it this way?
- What happens to it after use? How long will it last?

Evaluation – according to criteria and state why
- What effect will this product have on people's lives and relationships?
- Is this a better product than . . .?
- Is this a more important invention than . . .?
- Is this a more appropriate solution than . . .?
- What is wrong with this product?
- Why is this product not as popular as . . .?
- What could be done better or differently?
- How good is this product compared to . . .?
- What difficulties do users find with this product?
- What difficulties do manufacturers have making this product?
- What negative impacts does this product have on other people?
- Why have these particular ingredients been chosen?
- Can it be part of a sustainable world?
- Where do the ingredients come from?
- Is there a problem with side-effects?
- What else could have been used?

Classroom provision

Developing higher levels of thinking and metacognition

The key to understanding the world around us is to really observe the minutiae of objects in order to understand how they are made, why they are the way they are and how they actually work. Inspiration comes through knowledge.

(Paul Turnock, Brunel University School of Engineering and Design, www.brunel.ac.uk/about/acad/sed)

More able pupils benefit from activities in a scheme of work that ensures intellectual challenge – higher order thinking, reflection, exploring a variety of views, considering difficult questions, developing individual opinions, and connecting past and present learning. Planning should focus on high-quality teacher/pupil interaction with both teacher and pupils playing a range of roles – questioning, explaining and challenging.

'Thinking Actively in a Social Context' (TASC) provides a useful planning framework for D&T, as shown below.

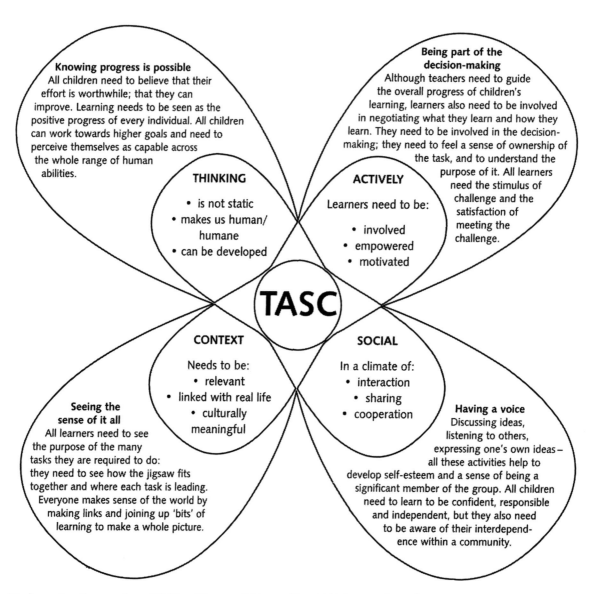

Mind mapping: the meaning of TASC and its essential tenets (from B Wallace *et al.* 2004)

Case study 8 – Year 7 Carry It All

Using case studies of designers at work

Teachers often use case studies that are linked to the current design brief, but for more able pupils you can choose case studies that are more unusual, thought provoking and encourage original thinking. These may include:

- inspiring designers – how they got their ideas

- new and interesting technologies

- showing the relationship between what pupils do in school and how products are designed and made.

For example, in this project on 'Carry It All' pupils are introduced to some hi-tech ideas about how a carrying device might be designed and used. This heightens expectations and moves pupils' ideas away from the well-known carrying devices – bags and boxes – to a different level. Pupils can be genuinely encouraged to consider how existing products make a difference to people's lives – to a lesser or greater extent. An activity such as looking at case studies, then asking pupils to rank the products in order from those making the most positive difference to people's lives to those making least . . . will provoke higher level thinking. An example of this activity and another 'How good is this product?' are included on the CD.

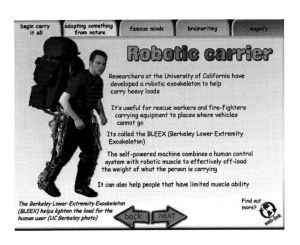

During the same project, the teacher also asks some pupils an open question about 'why worry about the environment' with some suggested website research and activities that they can do to help them consider the deeper issues surrounding their design ideas.

The teacher also used a card game – 'Get a Green Card' – to help the pupils assess the environmental impact of their design ideas in more depth (see further information of activities in the next chapter and on the CD).

The teacher gave the pupils a stack of green, red and amber cards or coloured blocks and then a series of statements:

- You have reduced the amount of material being used.
- You are making the product from materials from recycled products, such as glass, paper, aluminium foil or clothes.
- The materials you are using for your product will be recyclable in their turn.

- You have thought about what will happen when the product is thrown away.
- You have designed it so that parts such as fastenings or packaging can be used again and it is easily taken apart.
- You have reduced the amount of waste there might be during the making of the product.
- You have chosen or changed your materials and resources so that they are ones that will not run out or have side-effects.
- You have designed your product to use less energy.
- Your product encourages people to consume fewer resources.

If the pupils had already incorporated this into their design, they picked up a green card; if they had thought about it, or are thinking about doing it, they picked up an amber card; if they cannot do this for their product or design idea, they picked up a red card.

A quick glance at the coloured cards they have collected will give them an indication of how much they have considered the issues. They then consider how they can improve their design or product, eliminating the red and amber cards.

Don't stop at the project; always encourage the student to use other interests, perhaps incorporating other subjects, e.g. if a student has an interest in maths and physics, also encourage them to use this in the project, for example by considering forces applied.

(Ruza Ivanovic, Audi Young Designer finalist)

Adapting things from nature

An extension activity for the 'Carry It All' project would be to look at how solutions in nature can be used as a stimulus for design ideas and solutions (see further information on the CD). The idea is that pupils are asked to make connections across objects, contexts, users, materials and processes that they might not have thought about. There are many examples of how designers in the past have used nature as an inspiration for ideas, solutions and inventions, such as the hip bone being an inspiration for the design of the Eiffel tower, King Emperor penguins providing an insight into technical fabrics to withstand the cold weather, shark and seal skin to develop extra fast swimming costumes, the ability of leaves to wash dirt off naturally for new self-cleaning paint for external surfaces, studying the gecko's capacity to cling upside down to provide a new idea for a non-sticky, but ultra-strong tape.

These fascinating stories can encourage more able pupils to draw on a wider range of sources for design ideas and possible solutions, to make connections in usual ways or think outside the box. Simply by looking at these possibilities may inspire new questions for the pupil, to lead them in a new direction.

Give students more freedom to express themselves and encourage creativity.

(Julie Crawford, Audi Young Designer finalist)

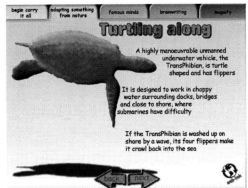

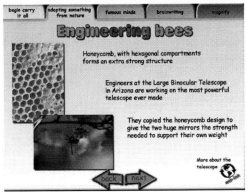

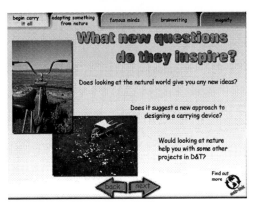

Designing things from nature

Case study 9 – Year 7 Soups and Salads: 5 a Day

In a project on salads, the teacher was concerned that the more able pupils' design ideas did not really reflect their capability because they were choosing an easy option. Their salad ideas were not very original and were limited by the kinds of meals the pupils had already eaten (typically lettuce, tomato and cucumber based). They were struggling to move beyond what they knew and were familiar with.

> I sometimes think about a project starting with a nonsensical statement. For example, if my problem is to design a car, the statement might be . . . The car has no wheels . . . Using this as a beginning, I arrive at solutions from another angle, even though my car may have wheels again.
>
> (Stefan Sagmeister, designer)

The teacher asked them to do an activity using 'nonsense statements'. These statements deliberately take the opposite view to what you would expect and challenge pupils thinking and assumptions. Here are some sample nonsense statements:

- this salad has no raw ingredients

- this salad has no vegetables in it

- this salad is not for the summer

- this salad is not for a 'slimmer'

- this salad is not green

- this salad is not a meal

- this salad is not cut up into pieces.

 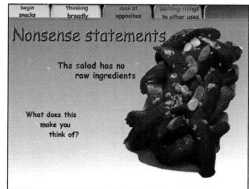

Nonsense statements

The pupils came up with far more creative and interesting thoughts. This technique is about:

- having fun and playing to be original

- turning assumptions upside down to clear a path to be innovative and inventive

- getting out of your box! Being daring!

- sharing risk by working together.

Nonsense statements can be written for a wide range of contexts and products, and pupils can be asked to add their own for future classes.

Case study 10 – Self- and group evaluation

How well am I doing – setting my own targets?

Most teachers ask pupils to complete self-evaluation forms and extend this to ask pupils about their own targets for the next project. Understanding progress during a project is very important. Sharing work and getting feedback on design ideas is very helpful for all pupils. A teacher may be able to offer some individual feedback on ideas, but this is difficult with large classes. But the group can be encouraged to comment on each other's work and help each other move their ideas forward and improve. In recent research by Goldsmiths University Technology Education Research Unit (TERU) for QCA, when they asked pupils about things that helped them move forward with ideas, all pupils said that getting feedback from their peers and sharing ideas was the most valuable activity that they did. Being part of a community of learners supports more able pupils.

This can be done during a 'group crit', '50–50', or 'On a scale of one to ten' activity. These techniques are meant to be purposeful, constructive, but interactive and a bit more interesting than a worksheet! A teacher can also enlist the help of an outside expert or mentor to support these activities.

A **group crit** can take place at a regular point in a project. Pupils take it in turns to present their ideas in a small group. They are asked:

- What is right about their ideas and project?

- What are the weaknesses?

- Are they solving a real problem?

See 'Your Best Bits' and 'Group Crit' on the CD for further detail.

A **50–50** activity is where pupils present a few of their design ideas and then ask others to rate them according to whether they think they will be successful or not (see further information on the CD). Ideas can be rated as:

- long shot

- 50–50

- possible chance

- likely

- excellent.

Just because an idea is rated as a 'long shot', it is not dismissed or considered to be a failure. The group then considers how to move an idea up the ratings. Often the long shot ideas will be the most interesting and encourage pupils to take risks.

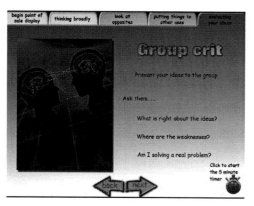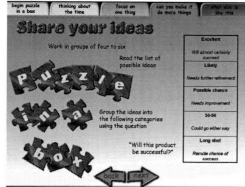

The group crit and 50–50 techniques

On a scale of one to ten ask pupils to simply assess how well they are doing with their ideas and what they need to do to get better. They give themselves a score on a scale of 1–10 for where they are now with their design ideas. They then think about what they need to do to improve their score. They may have one or two ideas for improving their work, and one or two problems that they identify they need help with. They are encouraged to get ideas from their classmates to help them. It empowers learners to focus on their individual needs, to make use of their strengths and recognise their weaknesses (see CD for further information).

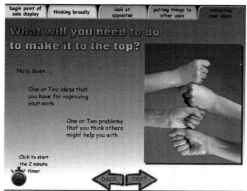

The 'on a scale of one to 10' technique for rating yourself

Case study 11 – Reflecting on learning

It is important to allow some time to reflect on the activity or the designing strategy used. Pupils can consider how they might apply it in the future and in another context. They can think about whether or not they found it a helpful strategy, if it suited their learning style and what they learned from it.

After pupils have been shown a particular strategy, for example – adapting things from nature, 50–50, nonsense statements, product evaluation, debates, word association, web research into history and product case studies – plan to ask a number of questions that encourage reflection of learning:

- What do you think of the strategy that you have just used to generate (develop) design ideas?

- Did this particular strategy help you come up with some new ideas?

- Did you get a lot of ideas? Were these ideas good ideas?

- How did the activity feel? Did it work for you?

- Is it similar to another activity? How did they compare?

- Would you use this activity again? In what project?

- What sorts of projects could you use this activity in?

- When would this activity help you?

- When do you think designers might use this kind of activity?

Students are encouraged to reflect on how well the strategy they have just used works for them

Encouraging independent learning and decision-making

Design is not like maths or science where there is only one correct answer; with design there can be many creative solutions to one problem. To produce great work you not only need talent but confidence to suggest solutions that are not the expected ones. The value of encouraging pupils to believe in themselves cannot be underestimated.

(Bruce Duckworth of Turner-Duckworth, www.turnerduckworth.com)

Decision-making is a skill that needs to be nurtured, developed and stimulated by providing pupils with appropriate situations, resources, stimuli and environments. Some ways that we can support pupils in D&T are:

- showing pupils that designing and making is a continuous decision-making process (for example, as the class looks at the possibilities, consequences, constraints and intentions)

- making decisions visible for pupils

- modelling examples of decisions made by others and the techniques they used to make effective decisions (for example where the project brief is set by the teacher)

- allowing pupils to make decisions (for example, where the project brief is chosen by the pupils) and experience the consequences of their decisions

- providing a structure for pupils to practice making decisions, beginning with simple choices and progressively dealing with complexity.

Progression in decision-making

Our more able pupils need to be provided with engaging activities that introduce strategies to help them to make decisions . . . **to be decisive** (in the true meaning of the word) – a range of opportunities to develop an understanding of what it means:

- to make choices and select 'carefully'

- to draw conclusions

- to come to a verdict of judgement based on what they know at that time

- to resolve issues that might conflict

- to assess and evaluate alternatives or options

- to examine their own preferences

- to justify something that is 'well chosen'

- to understand the decisions of others.

And consequently, these activities also teach them that designing and making is a continuous decision-making process. And that as they generate ideas, explore contexts and users' needs, develop ideas further, modelling, making and improving, that they need to understand **the place of indecisiveness:**

- hesitancy

- irresolution

- uncertainty

- vacillation

- fluctuation

- wavering.

The activities should provide them with strategies to consider simple and complex decisions and distinguish between the big and small decisions they face as designers. It helps them to understand that there are big decisions that affect people's lives for them to grapple with and make a difference to their world. Small decisions about how they might approach an activity, so that they can follow designing style that feels comfortable for them and deliver the same results as another way. And finally that every decision is transitory and developmental, to help them move onto the next stage and the next decision. But at some points, they have to apply their judgement and reconcile conflicting demands to come to a solution, and that they bring themselves and their values and beliefs to that decision. No decision is the wrong one unless you lose sight of who you are along the way.

The table overleaf sets out processes and strategies, taken from the Key Stage 3 strategy Module 4 Designing, for decision-making for 11–14-year-olds. An extended paper on teaching pupils decision-making in D&T is included on the accompanying CD.

Examples of strategies to teach decision-making

> Don't let them have an easy ride. They should motivate themselves but if not push them.
>
> (Jenny Andrews, Audi Young Designer finalist)

Unpacking a design brief

It is sometimes helpful to break the problem statement/brief/theme down into its component parts and to consider each in turn.

Design and make assignment – Corporate Identity

Souvenirs and collectables, e.g. T-shirts, 3D signs and models are used to promote events, pop stars, cartoon characters and even schools. Design and make a coordinated range of promotional products for a special occasion or a client. You should work in a team and produce at least three different products using a range of materials.

For example, a teacher uses this activity to 'unpack' a design brief with the pupils. Modelling aloud their thinking, the teachers underline the keywords or

Decision-making for 11–14-year-olds

Process	Decisions for Year 7 (11–12 years)	Decisions for Year 9 (13–14years)	Strategies
Exploring ideas and the task Pupils need to explore the needs, wants and opportunities within a task. By researching and questioning, using a variety of techniques (including ICT), they should gather information that helps them to clarify the task and exactly what they are required to do. As a result they should begin to envisage possibilities and to formulate criteria as part of a design specification. By reflecting on the needs and wants of users pupils should see how they can make creative interventions to improve quality of life, participate in tomorrow's rapidly changing technologies and help shape communities.	• What are my needs, wants and opportunities in this context? What shall I explore? • What are the design possibilities? • What constraints are imposed by the task? • What information shall I collect?	• What are the needs, wants and opportunities for others in this context? What shall I explore? • How can I explore conventional and unconventional ideas? • What should take priority? • What is the information I have collected telling me? Do I think it is right?	• Role-play • keywords • Moodboards • Mind mapping/ brainstorming • Big and small questions • Observing people and products • A day in the life of. . . .
Generating ideas Pupils should be taught to use the information gained from exploring the needs, wants and opportunities in the task, to analyse it further and to suggest what might be made in order to respond to design criteria. The study of products made by others could help this process. They should be taught a variety of techniques to stimulate the imagination and to develop their creativity. They should be encouraged to be flexible and independent in their thinking and to question, explore and play with their ideas mentally, verbally, graphically, in 3D and through the use of ICT. They should also be encouraged to be open-minded to different ways of working, to share their ideas with others and to offer and accept critical feedback. They should also be taught to see and make connections and relationships between products and ideas.	• What strategies can I use to generate a wide variety of ideas? • What can I do to stimulate my imagination? • How can I use the information the teacher has given me?	• How can I produce creative solutions? • What risks can I take? What techniques will help me? • Can I combine ideas from a variety of sources?	• Alternative uses • New from old • Extending the product range • Modify the . . . • Look to the future • Deconstruction • Walk on the Wild side
Developing and modelling ideas Developing ideas involves pupils in combining different design skills in order to move their thinking forward. This will usually involve them in modelling their proposals in a variety of ways, including verbally, in writing, graphically, by using ICT and in three dimensions. They will play with ideas whilst keeping their options open and create, recreate and interpret those ideas in both expected and unexpected ways. They will refine their ideas to develop a definite proposal that can be tested against the original design criteria. This may involve discussions with clients and users. They focus on their initial ideas, and parts of their initial ideas, working out the technical details, materials and manufacturing processes, which will be necessary to turn them into reality. As a result produce a detailed manufacturing specification.	• How can I explore and experiment with ideas before making judgements? • How can I explore and experiment to choose appropriate materials and processes?	• How can I try new approaches? • How can I use technical information to help me decide if a material or process is suitable?	• 12-minute discussion • 4×4 • Beg, steal or borrow • Champions • Prototyping and modelling • 3-minute sketching • SCAMPER

Planning

Pupils should be taught the principles of effective time and resource planning and management. This will need to include consideration of how to use time effectively, to sequence events, to decide on resources (including ICT), materials and processes, to utilise knowledge from other subjects where appropriate, and to reconcile the constraints imposed by costs and the availability of resources.

As the key stage progresses they will take increasing responsibility for their own learning and will develop skills that help them to work, and plan, individually and in teams of various sizes.

- How long will this short task take?
- Which short tasks can I manage independently?
- What am I responsible for? Which decisions can I share with teachers and others?

- How much time will I need to carry out the main stages of making?
- Carry out Design and make assignments in negotiation with the teacher, and prepare and follow own design briefs
- Which tasks will I need help from the teacher?

- Sequencing
- Consequence diagrams
- Flowcharts
- Production line

Evaluating

Evaluation will take place continually throughout the designing and making process. It allows pupils to make judgements or decisions about aspects of a design as it develops and to reflect on the strengths and weaknesses of a product once it has been completed. Pupils need to be taught how to analyse and explain their design decisions and the thinking implicit in products, processes and systems made by themselves and others. Analysing and evaluating past and present products and their effects on society will assist in the development of skills associated with evaluation. Discussions with the users of these products will also help this process, and help pupils to become discriminating and informed users of products. Over the key stage pupils should develop an initial understanding of the competitive nature of the design world. They should also develop their capacity to identify and critique the values underlying the intentions, design, manufacture and consequences of any such technology on themselves and others.

- How original and valuable are my ideas. Which ones are worth further development?
- What need does the product serve and how well does it meet that need?

- How will my ideas and solutions benefit individuals and the community?
- How could I judge the quality of a product and how far it meets the need, purpose and resource limits, and judge its impact on society?

- Thinking hats
- ACCESS FM
- Ranking
- Look from a different angle
- Right angle
- Gallery
- Compare and contrast
- Product pairs
- Product questions

Making

Pupils combine practical skills with an understanding of aesthetics, social and environmental issues, and function and industrial practices. Pupils demonstrate skills in creating products, processes and systems that achieve consistent production outcomes. They apply these skills in enterprising and empowering ways to personal and group situations. Pupils apply their knowledge of the characteristics of materials and equipment in creating solutions and designing to meet criteria related to function, aesthetics, sustainability and manufacture.

- What materials and components will I use? How accurate do I have to be? How will I pay attention to the quality of finish and to function?
- How well does my design work, bearing in mind the way the product will be used?

- What tools, materials, equipment and processes will I use and what are their characteristics?
- How will I check my work as it develops and modify in the light of progress?

- Group crit
- Matrices
- Beg, steal or borrow
- Champions
- Prototyping and modelling

Adapted from the 2003 DfES/KS3 National Strategy Pilot Framework for teaching design and technology: years 7, 8 and 9, and training module 4.

Classroom provision

phrases, such as souvenirs, collectables, promote, events and coordinated. They then take each keyword in turn and come up with as many alternative words as possible, for example for keyword 'souvenir' the teacher listed recall, takeaway, physical memory, keepsake, memento and reminder. The objective is to broaden the student's view of the design brief to the maximum. This strategy can be easily linked to brainstorming or mind mapping. An example activity is included on the CD to show you how to do this ('It's all part of the problem' worksheet).

A day in the life of . . .

Designers use this strategy to understand users' lives and to help them think of products that might be needed and the context that they are used in.

- Using a disposable camera, a person records a typical day in their life. Photographs are taken every hour and the photographer never appears in the photos.

A day in the life of . . .

Attribute	The character (the photographer)
Name and age	
Occupation	
Family situation	
What country? Where?	
Hobbies and interests	
Key values	

Design Museum CPD Designers in Action/IDEO Design Consultancy

- In groups, pupils discuss and record notes on a crib sheet using headings such as:

  What are their hobbies?
  What do they value?
  What do they read?

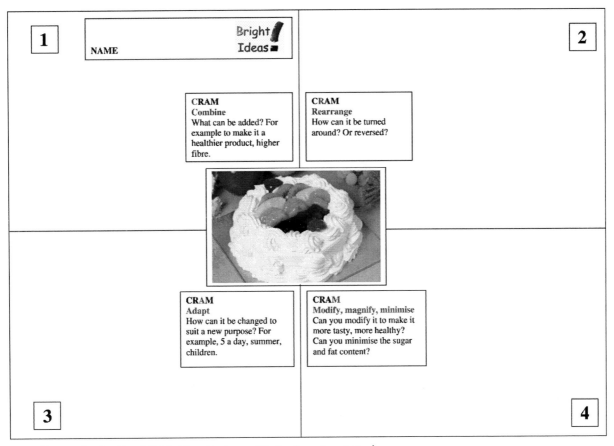

CRAM (from LT Davies, *Year 8 Bright Ideas*, Design and Technology Association)

- In the feedback it is important to question what clues the pupils used, and whether their assumptions are accurate or merely stereotypical views.

- This information can then be used to design products for that person, based on their interests, hobbies, reading, etc.

A sample 'Day in the Life' PowerPoint presentation, and a further explanation of the activity is included on the CD. The open response and different contexts that can be shown using this strategy make it ideal for more able pupils. It is an excellent activity to get pupils to take their own photos and makeup presentations.

4×4 group development of ideas

Four ideas from four minutes each is represented by '4×4'. Give out A3 sheet to all pupils. The sheet is divided into four, with a fifth space in the centre (see CRAM template and 4×4 further information on the CD provided).

Each pupil has four minutes to draw and annotate one of their design ideas and then passes the sheet to the next pupil in the group. They then have one minute to 'read' the drawing and three minutes to develop the orginator's ideas in the top left-hand space on the sheet – remember to consider materials and construction. After four minutes the sheets are passed around to the next member of the group and the process repeated in the top right-hand space. This continues until the sheet arrives back at the originator with four developments of the initial idea.

The originator can then review the four developments and select and reject these suggestions. It can help a pupil make decisions about the materials, processes and details of their design.

Providing a stimulating environment for the more able

Resources

Schools and departments need to assemble a range of study support activities and materials for both pupils and teachers. It may be possible to set up a resource centre within a school that is available to different groups of pupils at different times. Pupils should have access to reference books such as research and source materials for designing and revision guides, information books about topics and books of recreational skills development. They should also have the use of other materials to enhance learning and enjoyment of design and technology including videos, resources for practical tasks and investigative work and puzzles and games. Teachers need a range of resources on which to draw when planning lessons and tasks for pupils, including reference books that will assist them in increasing their own understanding, books outlining approaches to teaching particular topics, a range of textbooks, and photo-copiable activity sheets. The internet is a valuable source of information, ideas and resources for enhancing the teaching of design and technology.

Computers are an important resource for pupils of all abilities, but they are particularly useful when making provision for gifted and talented pupils, since they can be used independently in lesson or free time, or at home. Pupils can be encouraged to make use of a variety of computer resources including:

- an Integrated Learning System, which allows each pupil to work at his/her own level and rate, and monitors progress

- a range of CD-ROMs such as databases of materials, revision programs and games for extension or enrichment work

- the internet to research topics and activities

- computer programs such as CAD, spreadsheets and databases to develop and extend their work and enhance presentation.

Whilst computers are used in the D&T industries, this is by no means the solution to understanding design principles. It is merely a tool and should be regarded as such. Design is all about finding a solution to a problem; it is therefore the designer's task to illustrate and develop clear thinking skills and be able to present them clearly and effectively.

(Donna Fullman, Design Director of Eyefood, www.eyefood.net)

Communication and collaboration between teachers

Whatever provision is made for the most able pupils in any age group there is a need to avoid pupils repeating work that they have covered in earlier years unnecessarily and to build on prior knowledge and skills. Recording and communication systems need to be set up to ensure that, as far as possible, teachers are aware at the start of each year of the potential and levels of achievement of the pupils they will be teaching, the topics that they have covered and the resources that have been used. This is particularly important when pupils move from one school to the next. Effective communication and collaboration between teachers within individual schools, between primary and secondary teachers and between secondary and tertiary teachers is crucial if suitable provision is to be made for gifted and talented pupils to build on their achievements and progress at an appropriate rate throughout their school career. It is particularly important to ensure that communication systems exist, which facilitate the exchange of information between teachers when pupils move from one school to another. Primary teachers may benefit from the opportunity to discuss aspects of the curriculum for gifted and talented children with a design and technology specialist from secondary schools.

Consideration might also be given to creating opportunities for gifted and talented pupils from different schools to work together. In some cases secondary schools or colleges may be able to arrange masterclasses or activity days for pupils from their feeder schools. Alternatively, primary or secondary schools within an area might cooperate in establishing local networks with the aim of providing interesting and challenging activities and resources for gifted and talented pupils.

Team-teaching with teachers sharing expertise and learning from each other can be beneficial. It might also be possible for a specialist teacher to work with teachers in different classes taking lessons with the class teacher or working with particular groups of pupils to disseminate subject knowledge and good practice.

Teachers in secondary schools could give some consideration to how they might work with teachers in other subject areas to provide challenging projects for gifted and talented pupils. For example, design and technology can be a valuable source of interesting tasks that would allow able pupils to develop their mathematical skills through solving real problems.

Summary

What do gifted pupils dislike? Advice from a Northern LEA's guidelines:

- being made to feel different
- being expected to do extra work if it's more of the same
- low level tasks and time-filling activities, e.g. colouring in

- too much independent learning
- not being told the lesson objectives
- unhelpful marking, e.g. 'good' without giving reasons why
- overemphasis on writing – writing for the sake of it
- lack of variety in class work and/or homework
- always having to help people who didn't understand
- having to work at the same pace as everyone else and having to wait until everyone in the class understands before being able to begin work
- not being allowed an 'off day'.

What works? Deborah Eyre summarises good practice:

- Create a classroom climate that supports the development of high achievement – risk-taking, high-flying.
- Approach lessons as part of an apprenticeship in a subject, not just learning the knowledge and skills needed to pass the exam – a community of learners.
- Focus on the needs of individuals, make use of their strengths and recognise their weaknesses – empower learners.
- Design tasks that ensure intellectual challenge – higher order thinking.
- Focus on high-quality teacher/pupil interaction with both teacher and pupils playing a range of roles – questioning, explaining, challenging.

CHAPTER 6

Support for learning

> The most talented pupils need to be challenged to be inspired, they need to see other people's great work and want to be as good themselves. Designers are as competitive, to be the best, as any professional. Nurturing this competitive spirit inspires designers.
>
> (Bruce Duckworth of Turner-Duckworth, www.turnerduckworth.com)

There are many ways that teachers can support the learning of more able pupils. Resources have been developed for teachers to use alongside existing classroom activities, exam specifications and schemes of work. Descriptions of the major schemes available are included in this chapter.

These resources engage pupils in a range of ways.

- They provide depth in a particular issue that pupils can then pursue to their level, for example complex issues to do with sustainability, social and economic issues, the ethics of designing, considering how to improve the quality of life for others.

- They support pupils in developing technical skills and knowledge in a particular area of interest, for example food science, nutrition, engineering.

- They provide case studies and projects based on real scenarios to heighten expectations of pupils.

- They provide mentoring, outside experts and judges to allow pupils to work at the highest level.

Deborah Eyre recommends personalising learning through a blended approach:

- formal and informal academic learning opportunities

- 'home school' and beyond 'home school' provision

- local peer group and national peer group involvement

- 'applied experts' and 'experts' teaching

- face-to-face and online opportunities.

> Young designers just think about being a star and making money. They forget their duty to society. Everything you do must be in relation to your civilisation, your society, yourself, your life: without that the objects you make are just objects.
>
> (Philippe Starck, French designer)

The Sustainable Design Award

www.sda-uk.org

Intermediate Technology Development Group (ITDG) and the Centre for Alternative Technology and Loughborough University have worked in partnership to develop the Sustainable Design Award (SDA). The SDA is a freely available scheme for students and teachers. It is intended to help bring issues of sustainability into mainstream designing and making at AS and A2 level. It could be used with Key Stage 4 pupils who are starting AS courses in Years 10 or 11.

Exam boards have given greater emphasis to issues of environmental, economic and social sustainability in all parts of their syllabuses in recent years – the scheme offers teachers support in dealing with these issues, especially in relation to product analysis and major projects.

The award is part of the existing A/AS Level structure and is challenging for able pupils because:

- they work on genuine case studies and product studies within a variety of worldwide contexts – some northern hemisphere-based, others southern – and as these contexts are beyond most pupils' everyday experiences they are particularly stretching

- they address the complex issues of sustainability, appropriate design and manufacture

- they explore environmental, economic, social and moral issues in D&T and can pursue their own interests and capabilities

- they have access to tutors, mentors and study weekends throughout the project

- they have additional assessment criteria to meet

- they are rewarded with a high-profile awards presentation.

The award is available in product design, food technology, textiles technology, graphics, and systems and control. Teachers in over 300 schools in England and Wales have already undertaken it. For teachers there are training days held in June and July every year.

Case study – Nick Taylor

A guitar made from recycled plastics

Nick, an A2 student from Caistor Grammar School, started from a Loughborough University design brief suggesting possible uses of recycled polymers. One of the suggestions was to design and make a musical instrument. When Nick suggested it to his teacher, it was suggested it might prove overcomplicated. He was not deterred. He gained a lot of feedback from Eddie Norman, Senior Lecturer at Loughborough University and decided to use a sheet of recycled polymer made from yoghurt pots. Thanks to some guidance from Caistor's technician, Brian Clamp, Nick's work can be both seen and heard. It is a tribute to his determination, and to his ingenuity, that he has managed to produce an instrument of such high quality.

SDA – resources to use

Whether or not teachers and students chose to take part in the SDA scheme, there are free resources such as design briefs, supporting notes and eco-design tools for everyone to use.

Example design briefs

1. Reduce, reuse, recycle (UK)

Generic design brief

It has been recommended for many years that reducing, reusing and recycling provide many opportunities for environmental improvements in our own and other countries and in product manufacture. Design and make a product that uses at least one of those criteria.

Specific design brief

Cardboard has many fine structural properties and is finding uses as a building material. It is often made with recycled fibres. Use the structural properties of cardboard to design load-bearing furniture such as a bookcase or a chair.

Sustainability issues:

- Reducing the quantity of materials entering landfill sites can significantly reduce the environmental impact of people in the UK.

- The manufacture of an appropriately designed unit would provide worthwhile employment.

- Local manufacture of the product would provide employment in the UK and reduce transportation costs – both economic and environmental – associated with the product.

- Using recycled materials, reduces the extraction of raw materials and hence supports biodiversity.

2. Sustainable power (Kenya)

Generic design context

There are several sources of renewable energy. In many countries, micro-hydro power is a potential source wherever there is a reliable water supply. Investigate the appropriateness of micro-hydro power for an area of your choice and design and make a small machine that could harness that power for use in a small enterprise.

Specific design brief A: Product design – flour mill

Micro-hydro electric power has just been developed in the Kirinyaga area of Kenya. Flour is milled extensively using diesel and by hand at the moment. Design and make or model an electric flour-milling machine capable of being used by a small enterprise in the area. Consider the implications of scaling up in order to operate the machine in Kenya.

Specific example B: Product design – small machines

There are several other small enterprises that could be set up in the Kirinyaga area. Other possibilities include sunflower processing, welding, curing, cooking or carpentry. Design and make or model a machine suitable for any small enterprise in this area.

Sustainability issues:

- For many people in Kenya, developing ideas that would help them lead a more sustainable economic life is a priority. They do not lack ideas themselves but sometimes do not have the time or resources to be able to develop them. Your ideas could lead to greater economic stability for individuals or groups.

- Many items available in Kenya have been made overseas and imported. The aim of your project should be to develop a product that could be made locally using local skills, techniques and resources.

- Resources are scarce in Kenya, especially outside Nairobi. Designing and making that enables recycling or reuse of materials is therefore advantageous.

Ecodesign tools for students

www.sda-uk.org/toolsw.html

The Ecodesign web tool is a qualitative method of analysing products and can be used working in groups or individually.

Students can use the tool during product analysis to rate an existing product or design. It is also used to identify problem areas for design ideas. This indicates areas of the product that can be redesigned to improve its environmental sustainability.

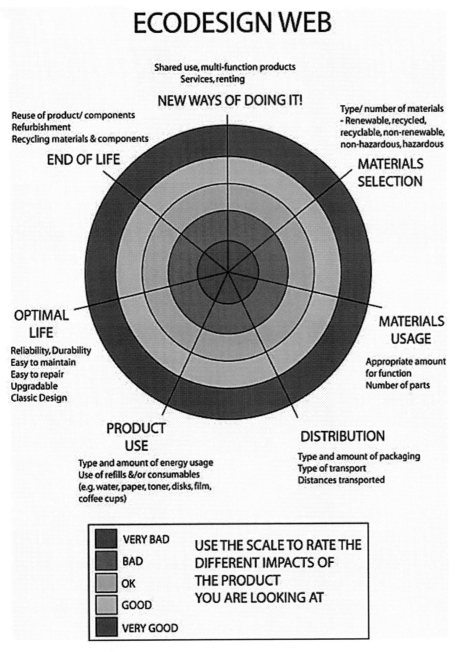

The Ecodesign web tool for product analysis

The Design Abacus

www.sda-uk.org/toolsa.html

A qualitative method of analysis used to identify areas for improvement, again can be used individually or as a group. Students can use the Abacus to rate a product on social, economic and environmental areas, in both the analysis and planning of a design. It is useful for comparing two products and can be marked up using two different coloured pens.

Eco-indicator

www.sda-uk.org/toolsi.html

This is a sophisticated tool as it is more detailed and ideal for more able students. It involves some qualitative analysis of products or designs allowing them to calculate their environmental and social impacts.

This tool requires students to take into account human health, ecosystem quality, the use of resources. They assess in detail the impact on different stages of the life cycle (production, use and disposal). This is done by producing a list of components and assessing the eco-indicator value of each product element. The higher the number of points, the worse the environmental impact. Students can then consider which elements and stages of the products life cycle cause most impact and can be focused on during redesign activities. The worksheet is provided in Appendix 6.1.

E-mentoring

E-mentoring is regular e-mail contact between an adult (who is not a teacher and not the parent) and a student. Many students benefit from getting advice about their design ideas or approaches from an expert outside of school, particularly to extend and challenge their thinking in further ways than the traditional classroom offer. This is particularly important if a design brief has been set by an outside company or the students need access to technical information and equipment that is not available in the school. E-mentoring overcomes the problems of when and where to meet and the costs and time involved in supporting students face-to-face. Many students are familiar with e-mail and messaging, so this offers a good alternative for them. It also helps develop the students' communication skills and offers a new approach to the use of ICT.

Case study – e-mentoring in the South East Oxfordshire Education Business Partnership

Fifty Year 10 and Year 11 students from four schools (Chiltern Edge in Sonning Common, Icknield Community Schools in Watlington, Gillotts in Henley-on-Thames and Langtree in Woodcote) volunteered to take part in a revolutionary mentoring scheme – e-mentoring in 2002.

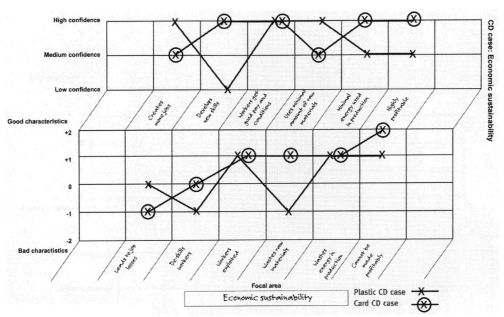

Using the Design Abacus to compare two types of CD case

The aim of the scheme was to enable students to discuss, via e-mail, issues that were important to them, with an adult who is not their parent or their teacher. This helped them to gain in confidence, receive individual support, gain a window on the world of work, and develop skills in communication, literacy, ICT, time planning and organisation.

The main objective of the scheme was to improve motivation and raise levels of achievement, as well as to create a culture of learning that enabled students to cope successfully with the pressures they face.

Businesses involved included Hewlett Packard, Yell Group, AIT, Invesco, Henley Management College, The River & Rowing Museum, Signals, Marbles and Consignia.

The school appointed a coordinator who identified the students/volunteers. Mentors were recruited via EBP and school contacts; students were matched after discussion between the students and the coordinator using a variety of matching processes.

The first e-mail was sent — a short pen portrait sent by the mentor to the school. The student then sent a similar portrait to the mentor — and the mentoring process began on a weekly basis, although in many cases this was more frequent.

All students and mentors met at least once per term. The initial meeting was at school, where the student was encouraged to show the mentor around the school — a great reminder to adults of what schools are like and how they have changed and are continuing to change.

The students were extremely enthusiastic — only one student out of more than 50 involved, dropped out. Attendance figures of some students dramatically improved, as did their attitude to school and schoolwork. Student evaluations indicated that they were more focused on their future and how they could improve their future job opportunities.

Comments from e-mentors

'The e-mentoring scheme is well worth while and challenging.'

'I feel that I am helping a student without having to make a huge commitment in terms of time or effort. I have got a lot more out of the scheme than I thought I would — I have learned perseverance!'

'I found it difficult to know if I was helping – and then I had an e-mail saying thank you for your help and support – it made me feel good, I'm keen to continue.'

Comments from students

'I'm enjoying e-mailing my mentor – it makes me feel important.'

'I find it hard to write the e-mails – but my mentor always writes back and I love getting the e-mails, so I make the effort to write back.'

'It's a good way of communicating with someone who has experience of the real life world of work.'

'I enjoy sending and receiving e-mails because I find it difficult to talk to adults face to face.'

Web broadcasting

Web broadcasting can be a good way of bringing mentors and experts to students. One example of effective use to support Key Stage 4 and post-16 students was the Dyson Web broadcast run by Dyson, Hertfordshire LEA and 3S Media. This came live from the Dyson premises and featured some of the company's leading design engineers talking about what they do and the process of developing a product through to manufacture. Students were able to view footage of Dyson products being developed, prototyped, tested and manufactured. They were able to e-mail questions to be answered by the design engineers during the broadcast.

The Science and Engineering Ambassadors programme

'The main purpose of the programme is to support teachers by enriching the curriculum and increase the number of young people with qualifications in science, design and technology, ICT and mathematics.'

Science and Engineering Ambassadors are volunteers with an interest in Science, Engineering, Technology or Mathematics (STEM), who are willing to work with schools, teachers and pupils to stimulate and inspire their interest in these subjects.

Science and Engineering Ambassadors (or SEAs) come from all walks of life and all sectors of the community. They may be practicing as scientists, engineers or technologists in a company or they may be people with a background and interest in those areas. What is important is that they are enthusiastic about STEM subjects and can communicate their interest and passion to pupils and young people.

As the Ambassadors are successful role models, they provide motivation and challenge more able students.

What does an Ambassador do?

Science and Engineering Ambassadors are people with science, technology, engineering and maths skills (STEM) employed in a variety of occupations.

SEAs are all individuals, with very different backgrounds and aspirations. As they are also volunteers their activities and the amount of time they can donate varies. However, examples of the type of activity with which they can assist include:

- helping with classroom projects on specific areas of expertise

- attending careers fairs and giving careers talks

- facilitating and mentoring groups on specific projects

- bringing an industrial perspective to STEM subjects and projects

- supporting out-of-school activities such as after-school clubs, challenges and competitions

- one-to-one mentoring of teachers and support teachers in lesson planning.

They have been briefed on working with schools and Criminal Records Bureau checked, so can offer valuable support in enhancing and enriching the curriculum, by providing a link from the classroom to the world of work.

You can find out about your local Ambassadors through SETNET or your local SETPOINT www.setnet.org.uk/cgi-bin/wms.pl/44. You will find further information in a PDF file on the accompanying CD.

Design and Technology Week

Design and Technology Week takes place in June each year. One of the key purposes is to celebrate pupils' achievements in design and technology through exhibitions of their work. Equally the week provides an opportunity for pupils to be involved in design and technological activities. The activities can range from specific challenges for year groups, to integrated cross phase work as part of an induction process to secondary school education. The QCA Key Stage 3 scheme of work has a unit of work designed for this purpose.

Design and technology week also brings schools in local areas or LEAs together, either to celebrate pupils' work or to publicise the subject.

Design and Technology Week can be used to suspend the timetable and focus on D&T for an extended period. More able pupils can benefit from the approaches used, and also the opportunity to get recognition for the talents through exhibition, awards, assembly, etc.

What type of activities can you do?

Here are some examples:

- design and technology challenge for whole year groups
- competition for pupils
- having a designer in residence
- having an engineer into school to work with pupils
- industry-based design and make activities
- mini-enterprise activities
- design and technology parents' day/evening
- industrialists in schools initiating challenges for pupils
- design and technology conference for teachers
- exhibition of work in school or in the local community
- visits to local companies
- visits to local museums or activity centres or Design Museum/Science Museum
- videoconferencing linked to a school overseas or in this country.

How do you organise Design and Technology Week activities?

There are many levels at which these activities can be arranged. At one level in your classroom or department you can have a focus during the week. This can be a common challenge surrounding a design and make activity, an exhibition of work open to parents and the local community or a linked activity with local schools.

The following key steps may be worth considering when setting up your activity:

- draft your ideas for an activity
- hold a meeting with colleagues in schools, or local schools, or with the LEA
- agree proposals and then develop an action plan to set up the event
- advertise the event
- seek sponsors if required
- plan venues and activities
- ensure local press, radio, television are invited to the launch
- publicise the outcomes of the event.

Further information can be found on the Design and Technology Association website at www.data.org.uk.

Young Foresight

www.youngforesight.org

> Meeting future needs demands a leap of imagination . . . it calls for hard-headed realism in assessing challenges that are, ten, twenty or fifty years down the line.
>
> (Tony Blair, Prime Minister)
>
> Young Foresight is about taking action now to prepare young people for the future!
>
> (Lord Sainsbury, Minister for Science and Innovation)

Young Foresight is an educational initiative for design and technology pupils in Year 9 (age 13/14) but has been used successfully with both older and younger pupils. It is a revolutionary project aimed at giving students direct experience in all the skills needed to create a successful product or services: from conceptualisation, to design, to adaptability in the marketplace. It is a complete resource for teachers with accompanying BBC films, website, teachers' notes, industry mentors and well-tested pupil activities (an example activity is on the CD – '4R's of creativity').

In Young Foresight, pupils, working in teams, design products and services for the future. Using new and emerging technologies for the basis of their designs they develop their own design briefs and specifications. They justify their design decisions by group discussions and class presentations. As a result they develop a wide range of communication skills, enhanced creativity and improved design ability.

The programme requires approximately one term (12 weeks), but can be adapted to take less time. For example:

- 24 × 50-minute sessions (approximately one term's work)

- 8 × 50-minute sessions (approximately four weeks' work)

- one-week intensive period (e.g. Design and Technology Week)

- one-day intensive period (e.g. induction days)

- lunchtime/after-school clubs (e.g. Young Engineers)

- gifted and talented summer schools.

Young Foresight principles

Young Foresight challenges the orthodoxy of design and technology practice in seven important ways. It does not do this lightly. Young Foresight believes current practice is limiting pupil's achievements and experience of technology.

1. Young Foresight requires pupils to **design but NOT make**. If pupils always have to make what they design this will limit their ambition to that which

can be achieved with the tools, equipment, materials and time available in school. Pupils will learn very little about modern technologies and the way they can be used if they can only engage with technologies available in school through designing **and** making. Pupil's creativity will be severely constrained by the need to make what they have designed.

2. Young Foresight requires pupils to **work as groups** in which all members contribute to generating, developing and communicating design ideas. In the world outside school, multidisciplinary teams design most complex products and services, and Young Foresight wants to put pupils in similar situations.

3. Young Foresight requires pupils to **design products and services for the future**, not for themselves or members of their family now, nor for probable immediate markets. It does this because it wants to give young people a stake in the future; a view about what it could be like and the contribution they can make by having ideas.

4. Young Foresight does not expect the teacher to tackle this task alone. Young Foresight helps schools find **ambassadors from industry** who can work in a variety of ways to support pupils designing for the future.

5. Young Foresight expects pupils to **use new and emerging technologies** as the basis for their design ideas. These are technologies that will not be available in school. Young Foresight does this because it believes the best way for young people to learn about technologies that will have a large effect on all our lives is for them to think about how they could be used.

6. Young Foresight requires pupils to **present their ideas** to their peers, their teacher and mentor, and to audiences at conferences on innovation. These presentations can vary from the informal and spontaneous – commenting on a handwritten flip chart – to the formal and well rehearsed – using a data projector linked to a short documentary drama.

7. Young Foresight requires pupils to **develop their own design briefs**. This is a much more open approach to that usually taken with pupils of this age. As a result they have to consider the needs and wants of people in a future society and the markets that might exist or could be created.

Case study – a weighing case

Ursline College, Westgate on Sea

The suitcase, which tells you how heavy it is, it uses QTC to measure the weight of the luggage so you know that it is within the weight limit when travelling.
   When you lift the suitcase by its handle QTC bellows deform under strain and a backlit indicator shows the weight of suitcase and contents.

Case study – clothes that change colour and pattern to music

King Solomon's School, Redbridge

A 'graphics' tablet worn on the sleeve uses the electrical signals generated by changes in pressure on QTC to display messages on a 'soft' screen in a T-shirt.

QTC in the soles of the trainers respond to the pressure patterns generated by dancing to give electrical signals that make the electrically sensitive dyes in the trousers become luminous.

The ultimate peacock!

Case study – pacemaker

Meoncross School, Fareham

Allows a pacemaker to alert changes in heart rates and regularity. QTC threads are attached to the heart to measure the stretch and regularity of the heartbeat. When the pacemaker receives a signal of irregularity it transmits a warning to a remote medical facility.

If irregular, the lack of pressure sends a message to the pacemaker.

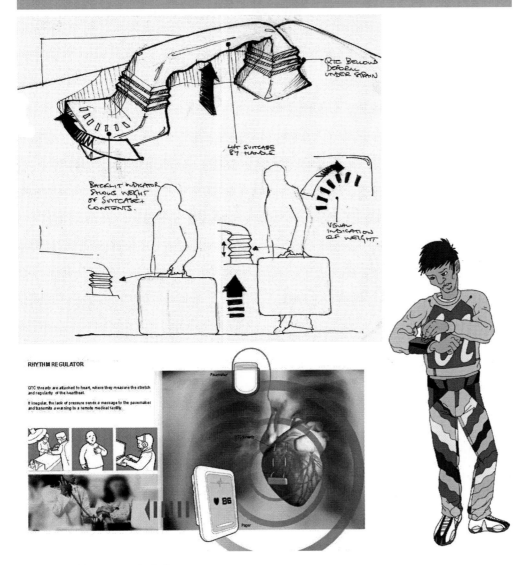

Young Foresight case study designs

Taste of Success

www.data.org.uk/secondaryfoodawards

The Taste of Success Awards is focused around the successful completion of a food brief by pupils aged 9 to 16 years. Sainsbury's Supermarkets Ltd, the Design and Technology Association (DATA) and the British Nutrition Foundation (BNF) developed them. They are supported in England by the Department for Education and Skills (DfES) and in Scotland by the Scottish Executive's healthy living campaign. A key focus of the food awards is practical work with food. In essence, the food awards encourage good work in food studies, including design, planning, preparation, making skills, presentation and evaluation by pupils of all abilities. The emphasis is to recognise and reward the excellent work already going on in schools – not to create additional paperwork or overload teachers with yet another initiative.

For each successful task finished, children will receive a certificate indicating that they have completed an award brief. The food awards reward and recognise your pupil's hard work – through what has to be taught at school.

Gold and Platinum Awards are suitable for the more able pupils and can be undertaken at any age.

In addition, online resources to support teaching are available at: www.j-sainsbury.co.uk/tasteofsuccess.

Gold Award briefs

Foods of the World
Develop a range of products that uses authentic ingredients from a country or region of your choice, e.g. Europe or Asia. Take one idea to prototype stage, emphasising its traditional aspect.

Catering for Health
Many school meal services rely on ready-made dishes or products, which can be heated and served quickly and conveniently. Make a range of meal options for a school canteen that follow current healthy eating principles, are capable of being successfully chilled and reheated, and have pupil appeal.

Specialist Diets
Develop a range of frozen meals, taking one through to prototype stage, which would be suitable for either:

- a person with intolerance to wheat or gluten, or

- a person with an intolerance to dairy products.

Gold Award requirements

To gain a **Gold Award** pupils have to meet the following criteria:

1. justification – evidence of literature support and survey work

2. planning and preparation – production schedule, including a specification

3. making skills – a range of advanced skills, including a range of equipment

4. safety and hygiene – implements basic HACCP procedures

5. presentation of final product – high-quality finishes applied

6. evaluation – systematic analysis and review of the production process.

To gain a **Gold Merit Award** pupils have to get a merit in four of the criteria listed.

Platinum Award briefs

Salt and Health

In 2003 the Government's Scientific Advisory Committee on Nutrition (SACN) published a report on 'Salt and Health'. This report sets targets for salt intake for children, as well as adults. Develop a dish that:

- is lower in salt than traditional counterparts

- promotes vegetable consumption

- is aimed at children aged 7–10 years

- supports the SACN recommendations.

5-a-Day

A retailer is looking for an innovative savoury ready meal to add to their lower fat range. The meal should also encourage fruit and vegetable consumption. The meal should come under the category of Food from Around the World. Develop a dish that meets this criteria, plus:

- is between £1.49 and £3.99

- is 300g for a light meal and 450g for a main meal

- is less than 3% fat (with saturates being less than 50% and less than 450 kcals

- incorporates at least one portion of fruit or vegetables, so helping people towards 5 portions a day.

Food for All

A recent report by the British Nutrition Foundation suggests that as many as 20% of the population perceive themselves to have a food allergy or intolerance; however, current estimates suggest only 1–2% of adults have a true food intolerance and around 5–8% children. Eating a well-balanced diet can be tricky if you or a member of your family has a food allergy or food intolerance. These people strive to find alternatives to basic everyday food items and tasty treats/snacks. Design and make a tasty everyday bakery product that meets the following criteria:

- suitable for a person with intolerance to wheat or gluten

- made with minimum use of additives such as food colours

- packed with all the flavour and texture of a gluten/wheat containing equivalent product

- comparable cost with a gluten/wheat containing equivalent product.

Platinum Award requirements

To gain a **Platinum Award** the pupil has to meet the following criteria:

1. explores ideas through personal and desk research, which is appropriate to the brief and justified in its use

2. generates and develops a variety of ideas, showing appropriate application of research and food and nutrition knowledge

3. plan effectively to undertake practical work

4. demonstrate skilful use of a range of equipment, tools and ingredients

5. makes high-quality prototypes, samples, dishes or products

6. applies good personal hygiene practices

7. evaluates work throughout with regard to practical outcomes, sensory qualities, objective testing, nutritional analysis, cost and meeting original need.

To gain a **Platinum Merit Award** pupils have to get a merit in five of the criteria listed.

British Nutrition Foundation A Level awards

These annual awards are given for the pupil who gets the highest mark in the practical coursework project at A Level. There is one award for each awarding body.

In 2000, Sarah Kind, of Queen Elizabeth School in Horncastle won the BNF prize for highest marks in Edexcel A Level Food Technology coursework. By 2003 Sarah was in her second year studying part-time for a BSc in human nutrition and product development. After leaving school, Sarah started work with Somersby Foods as a Quality Assurance assistant. They sponsor her university study. She has already twice won the National Food Excellence Student award for best product development. In 2001 Sarah won the award for her gluten-free frozen ready meal 'Salmon Highlander' and the following year, Sarah won for her snack product 'Spicy Risotto Crunchies'.

In 2001, Amy Lee, of Westcliffe High School in Essex won the Award for Edexcel. In 2003, she was in her second year at the University of Surrey reading nutrition and dietetics. Amy's interest in the link between diet and health started during a project for her GCSE coursework. For this, she was asked to identify a diet or nutrition problem that required a particular food item and then create a new food product. Amy focused on restaurant foods suitable for pregnant women. After performing well in her GCSE, Amy continued to study at A Level. Amy's coursework focused on foods suitable for people with celiac disease. Her research showed a lack of variety of products and created new items, taking into account the nutritional requirements of her targeted markets. In a second piece of coursework Amy created healthy desserts for schoolchildren. While studying A Level, Amy shadowed a community dietician and decided that she would like to study to be one herself.

In 2002, Dipna Anand, from Heston Community College, Hounslow, won the highest marks for Edexcel. In 2003 Dipna was in her first year at Thames Valley University studying for a BA in Hospitality with Food Studies. Dipna's interest in food and diet was triggered after her father suffered a nonfatal heart attack. Dipna's father did not smoke or drink, but was told by specialists that his heart attack was the result of having a diet too high in fat. Dipna's father owns an Indian restaurant and ate a lot of high-fat curries. For her A Level coursework, Dipna created new recipes suitable for her father's restaurant, which had a reduced fat content. Among the lower fat dishes were Masala chicken with soya and stuffed mushrooms, and Masala fish with vegetable rice. As well as creating recipes, Dipna designed the packaging and conducted taste tests for each recipe.

Audi Innovation Awards

'Our logo-centric culture, TV images and the over-reliance on computer graphics is leading to a creative dumbing-down in children. Thinking in a linear fashion, over-use of technology in the early design stages, being exposed to pre-fab design "rules" – rather than taking creative leaps and risks – is threatening to displace much of the intuitive, spontaneous creativity inherent in our children. A child's early inclination to think outside the normal constructs must be protected – creativity needs to be fought for as an intellectual right. And to this end the Audi Innovation Awards are a wonderful initiative, encouraging true creative risk-taking at a key stage in a child's development.'

(Dr Aric Sigman, consultant psychiatrist)

This scheme provides valuable teaching support for D&T. The scheme aims to inspire creativity, stimulate imagination and allow minds to explore the wildest ideas among 11–14-year-olds. The resource sets six challenges from the design of a nutritious menu for a three-day exploration in space to the creation of a new

Olympic sport. A panel of teachers from England, Scotland and Wales devised the challenges.

> Young people possess such huge amounts of creativity, as well as the boundless energy and enthusiasm needed to take creative leaps and explore new concepts. The Audi Innovation Awards provide a context for young students to take these creative risks and to stretch their imaginations with fun challenges, which are relevant to their education.
>
> (Michael Farmer, Manager of the Audi Design Foundation)

The Audi Innovation Awards are open to all Design and Technology / Technology Education Key Stage 3 students (aged 11 to 14). They can enter individually or in groups of up to four. For example, these were the 2005 Challenges set:

- **Challenge 1 – If I were a spizzle . . . what would I be?** This challenges students to design a 'spizzle' – something that can be used by everyone, but cannot be bought in a shop.

- **Challenge 2 – Let there be light!** This challenges students to design a new torch that works without using the conventional on/off switch.

- **Challenge 3 – Space food challenge** This challenges students to create a nutritious, balanced and tasty three-day menu for astronauts to consume while in space.

- **Challenge 4 – Weather station challenge** This challenges students to design a range of protective clothing for a mission to Mars, taking into consideration the different conditions and atmospheres that the astronauts will encounter.

- **Challenge 5 – Out of this world challenge** This challenges students to design a new national sport and equipment to present to the Olympic committee for approval for inclusion in the next Olympic Games.

- **Challenge 6 Aqua-craft challenge** This challenges students to design a single-person vehicle that can be used both in water and on land. The source used to power the vehicle uses energy that no longer contributes to global warming.

The Spirit of Innovation Awards

This awards scheme in the north East considers innovative products and services.

The entries are reduced to 12 finalists in five categories – students of all ages, individuals over 18, small companies, large companies and an overall winner.

> Over the past five years the Spirit of Innovation Awards has unveiled great ideas for new products and services from more than 350 North East innovators and celebrated outstanding ideas from 22 winners. This year is certainly no exception and the vast range of applications we've seen once again proves that innovation really is alive and kicking in this region.
>
> (Frank Nicholson, business consultant and judging panel chairman)

Case study – Robert Orford, winner of the individual category and overall winner

Wheelchair users may soon benefit from greater independence if new technology to make moving around much simpler takes off.

Nineteen-year-old, Robert Orford from Gateshead, won the award with the design of 'EZ Wheel', his D&T A Level project. The EZ Wheel is a wheelchair propulsion aid, which allows wheelchair users to propel their chair forwards and backwards, turn on the spot and brake in a controlled fashion. It can also be used as a handbrake. The device consists of a pair of levers attached to the chair's axles. These drive the wheelchair via a pair of jammers positioned either side of the hand-wheels and can be controlled by a simple twisting action of the wrists.

The innovation makes propelling a wheelchair 40% easier and prevents the need to bend forward to reach the wheels, protecting hands from becoming trapped in wheel spokes or suffering abrasion from gripping hand-wheels during braking.

Case study – Richard Merriam, winner of the student category

An A level student at Yarm School, Richard Merriam invented an 'auto drinker' to allow people suffering from stroke, multiple sclerosis or muscular dystrophy to drink unaided. Richard came up with the idea as part of his A Level D&T course, when Neater Solutions Limited, a specialist in developing solutions for less able people, issued him with the design brief.

The objective of the 'auto drinker' is to supply drink to people with poor suction or none at all, who are unable to pick up a drinking vessel and need liquid to be pumped into their mouth. Products already available on the market are gravity fed, but this is the first design to include a pump.

The product uses a peristaltic pump, commonly found in kidney dialysis machines to pump liquid into a person's mouth. Around the pump, electronics control the function, an aesthetic shell enhances its appearance and a coaxial straw delivers drink into the person's mouth.

An interface panel fitted to the back of the device switches the power on and off and adjusts the time that the pump functions – anywhere between one and nine seconds. The pump releases 3.5ml per second. A 'Go' button is also included and when pressed, will deliver drink for the set period.

Young Engineers for Britain (YEB)

www.youngeng.org/about_yeb.html

Young Engineers for Britain and YEDA combined to form one national engineering and electronics design and technology competition.

This national competition is for students aged 11–19. Students design, invent and construct new ideas into marketable projects and inventions that solve a need in the community or industry. Students can work either as individuals or in teams of up to four students. Projects can include GCSE or A Level project work, can be part of a 'working in industry' award such as the Year in Industry or EES, or can be something that the student has a personal interest in and sees as a good idea. Students are selected from the 11 regional finals held throughout the UK. Many of the winners will be taken on international trips abroad such as the Intel International Science and Engineering Fair.

The challenge

Young Engineers for Britain and YEDA challenges students to use their imagination to create, design and develop an original idea for a commercially viable device or system that meets a useful everyday need they have identified, such as a sporting activity, hobby or task at work or in the home, or for people with special needs.

Taking part in the competition provides an opportunity to learn more about all aspects of engineering, electronics and ICT, as well as giving practical, technical and marketing experience, while having a lot of fun putting an idea into practice. This will put students in good stead for a future career in the industry.

Who can enter?

It is open to all 10–19-year-olds – at school, college, university, working in industry students or an industrial trainee, individually or as part of a team.

The process

- Identify an everyday task or social need

- Dream up a creative solution to address a bright idea

- Carry out market research

- Design and develop project and consumer test the idea for user reaction

- Create a design portfolio and photograph the project either complete or nearing completion, they may use their GCSE or A Level course work (a copy is fine)

- Entrants will be invited to a regional final.

- Consider protecting the project or idea with intellectual property rights and patenting.

Case study – Martin Rosinski

Fifteen-year-old Martin Rosinski of Ponteland Community College designed 'SMARTLINK' and won a prize for the most imaginative concept. SMARTLINK® is the world's smallest data logger, which is developed for stress measurement in the most difficult industrial applications where none of the existing measuring systems can be used.

YEDA 2000

Martin Rosinski

'SMARTLINK' ®

SMARTLINK® is the world's smallest data logger which is developed for stress measurements in the most difficult industrial applications where none of the existing measuring system can be used.

A very advanced firmware which I developed, combined with Infra-Red communication and specially developed Windows CE software, allows to start data acquisition and download the data from the rotating or reciprocating machinery during its normal operation.

These miniature data loggers were already used in many important industrial applications world-wide. Some of the applications included: Rail Axle stress measurements (used in Indonesia and Hong Kong), Leisure Industry and Automotive. Smartlink® was used to measure stresses in critical components of roller coasters and was fitted in Cedar Point (USA), Barcelona (Spain) and Alton Towers (UK). The operation of these units was verified in-service and recently on a specially developed test rig operating at 30000 RPM. Future applications include Helicopter Blade stress evaluation and Wind Turbine fatigue life assessment.

Smartlink® is now a registered design and a World licence is being negotiated with the globally operating PLC company.

Ponteland County High School
Callerton Lane, Newcastle NE20 9EY
Tel. 01661 824711

Martin Rosinski's SMARTLINK project

Case study – Saqib Shaikh

Saqib Shaikh of RNIB New College near Worcester designed Braille Magic, a Braille translator for Microsoft windows, which turns ASCII text into Braille output suitable for driving an embosser.

Martin Rosinski (left) and Saqib Shaikh (right) at the Young Electronic Designer Awards

Jaguar F1 Team in Schools CAD/CAM Design Challenge

www.f1inschools.co.uk/

The F1 Team in Schools Challenge is a competition, open to all UK-based secondary schools and colleges, to design and manufacture CO_2 powered model racing cars (dragsters). Student teams compete against each other in a national championship to determine the best-engineered and fastest car in the UK. The competition is run by F1 in Schools Limited – a nonprofit organisation – with backing from sponsors Denford, Jaguar and BAE Systems.

As well as the Jaguar F1 Team in Schools certificates, it is also possible to gain other awards, with the work done by students for the Challenge:

- The **Duke of Edinburgh Award** is split into five sections: Service, Skills, Physical Recreation, Expedition and Residential Project. The work done for the Challenge can be used as part of the 'skills' section of the Award. For those who enter this scheme, think creatively and make sure you keep a record of all your work using an activities log.

- **BA CREST** is a nationally recognised accreditation scheme for project work in the fields of science and technology. To receive an award, set hours of project work have to be completed and presented. The F1 in Schools portfolio work can be used to gain this accreditation.

- The **Year in Industry**, or YINI as it is also known, is a scheme for 'gap year' students who want to spend a year in industry before or during university. So after F1 in Schools students can take a year out in engineering before going to university.

Case study – applied engineering and the F1 in Schools Challenge

Gary Glover is a design and technology teacher at Sandhill View School, who has been involved in the challenge for the past two seasons, bringing teams to compete at regional and national level.

As part of the applied GCSE engineering course at Sandhill View School the pupils are required to produce an engineered product. In association with the City of Sunderland College, Gary attended a presentation by Heather Hawthorne on the Jaguar F1 Team in Schools CAD/CAM Design Challenge. Gary found that the Challenge met many of the requirements for the GCSE specification and at the same time was a 'real project', in the sense that there were prescribed criteria in the form of a technical design specification, along with a design brief. Taking this into account, Gary introduced the Challenge to the class and showed them the demonstration videos. Instant motivation!

Gary split the class into teams and started on the project. Teams worked individually and together to help ensure they would be successful in the competition and at the same time were producing portfolios of evidence for their GCSEs. As this teamwork continued, Gary found himself becoming more a facilitator than a traditional 'teacher'; as Gary says, 'The competition has made teaching the Applied Engineering course easier. No need to try and motivate pupils! No more missed teacher deadlines, no more excuses! Just clear evidence available for their Applied GCSEs – a practical "real engineering" project. Pupils can see why they are doing the work, appreciate the need to work in teams, individually as well as communicate with a variety of people at all levels.'

He would give help when necessary, but the group were already identifying their needs. It was no longer a course where he had to dictate every element. Pupils were motivated and competitive, wanting to get to the National Final in London. The teams were committed to producing quality work and products. Instant differentiation was achieved as the more motivated and competitive teams put more effort in and produced better work.

Gary has found and continues to find the competition to be a massive success for his pupils. The life skills they have learned and experiences they have gained he believes will be with them for the rest of their lives and at the same time they are getting GCSEs. 'What we wanted from this project was to raise achievement! The success the pupils have had has been highlighted in school, regionally (in local newspapers), nationally both via the F1 competition final and promotional work, and through the DfES breakthrough project – Raising boys' achievement.' said Gary.

Case study – F1 day at Frankley City Learning Centre

Frankley City Learning Centre (CLC) is one of a network of City Learning Centres across the UK providing technological support and training for local schools in their area and beyond.

Frankley CLC is based at Frankley Community High School in Birmingham and is a Jaguar F1 Team in Schools manufacturing, test and race centre. As part of the training, Frankley CLC organised an F1 in Schools day at the centre. This was an opportunity for five of their West Midlands schools to bring their F1 teams together to discuss their work, carry out testing on their designs and learn from the experience.

As well as all the other fantastic Computer Aided Design (CAD) and Computer Aided Manufacture (CAM) equipment, Frankley CLC also have a track and wind tunnel. Having this equipment meant that students were able to test the aerodynamics of their car, compare the performance of each other's cars and also able to race their cars for the first time. Val Allen, Frankley CLC, said 'Pupils from the five different schools came together for a brilliant day, which included learning about aerodynamics, testing their cars in the wind tunnel and racing their cars on the full-length track. Pupils new to the competition were able to learn from the more experienced teams. Portfolios and presentations were shared and the teams had time to work on these during the day. We were delighted that one of the teams represented on this day went on to win the Midlands Regional final.'

Case study – when the little dragsters got bigger . . .

While at school, Adam Charnley was a Jaguar F1 Team in Schools competitor. In 2002 his team won the Midlands final and finished second in the National competition. He is now an undergraduate at the Swansea Institute of Higher Education, where he is studying Motorsport Engineering.

Adam first became interested in motor sports at the age of 11, when his mother decided to take him to watch drag racing at Santa Pod in Northamptonshire. Santa Pod is the home of European drag racing, with cars reaching 300mph along the quarter-mile stretch. This sport is one of the fastest and loudest around. Adam was immediately 'hooked'.

When Adam's school became involved in F1 in Schools, Adam along with two other students decided to form their own team. 'My interest took another step up when I discovered a school competition called F1 in Schools.' Not only did Adam's team compete in the Challenge, but they turned out to be one of the top teams in the country. In the 2002–03 season they won their Regional Final and finished second at the National in January 2003.

Now at Swansea Institute of Higher Education studying Motorsport Engineering, Adam has decided to use some of the skills he learnt through F1 in Schools to make a slightly larger car! 'As part of my course I need to complete an engineering or design project relating to a racing car, so I decided to build my own dragster. To be truthful I'm building it because I want to!' Adam has now started to construct a 700bhp per tonne dragster! As well as constructing the dragster Adam has raised sponsorship from F1 manufacturing centre, Frankley CLC, where he gained valuable manufacturing knowledge from Bob Rose while completing work experience last year before starting university. Towards the end of the year, it is likely that the car will be launched.

Find out more at www.freewebs.com/cougarracing.

4×4 in Schools Technology Challenge

www.4x4inschools.co.uk

This team challenge is to design and build a remotely controlled four-wheel-drive vehicle that will negotiate challenging road surface obstacles and electronic tests, on a model off-road track that emulates the concept of a Land Rover.

The Process

Research:

- Use ICT

- Investigate 'web' information

- What makes a 4×4 different?

- What is the Land Rover concept?

- Remotely controlled commercial vehicles evaluation (teardown)

- Component suppliers.

Design a vehicle:

- using ICT – CAD

- based on documented research

- to a specification set by Land Rover Engineers

- incorporating commercially produced and self-build components

- including mechanical linkages, suspension, electronic and drive systems, etc.

Manufacture the designed vehicle using:

- ICT – CAM/CNC

- vacuum forming

- electronic solutions

- printed circuit boards.

Test and evaluate:

- the prototypes

- the manufactured vehicle against the specification and demonstrate the development.

Compete at regional and national finals:

- Each team is required to test their vehicle against the Land Rover 4×4 In Schools Test Track emulating the formidable Land Rover off-road test tracks.

- Each team is required to provide an electronic diary that clearly records the decision-making process and how that informed the design process.

- Each team is required to make a ten-minute presentation to Land Rover Engineers outlining their process and highlighting the design, technology and business acumen. The Land Rover 4×4 Challenge is supported by AQA and QCA.

Rapid Response Engineering Challenge

This challenge is a civil engineering problem solving activity based on the needs of an area after a natural disaster, e.g. a hurricane.

The Challenge:

- provides students with experience in handling uncertainty and responding positively to change

- encourages creative problem solving and implementation

- develops risk-management skills and an understanding of financial planning

- allows students to develop an understanding of the business context and make informed choices between alternative uses of scarce resources.

Case study – 2004 Hurricane Mitch Challenge

Tom Jarvis, Zipei Zhang, Ahmed Ahmed, Mohamed Ibrahim, Douglas Wood and Luke Roddis, all of Year 9, went to the Don Valley Stadium to compete in the Rapid Response Engineering Challenge for South Yorkshire.

They were sponsored by local construction company Gleeson and called themselves The Gleeson Gladiators. Equipped with hard hats and reflective jackets, they set about the challenges in front of them.

All the challenges were set in the aftermath of Hurricane Mitch, which destroyed large parts of Honduras in 1998. The team took on the role of Rapid Response civil engineers and had to address the key problems associated with provision of transport, shelter and sanitation in a disaster area. The morning exercises were based inside and culminated with the team delivering a presentation of their solution to the siting of an emergency encampment for the people of a devastated town. They had to take into account water supply, pick-up of emergency aid and best location for the shelters and toilets.

Going into the afternoon, the teams were challenged to construct a water supply system to transport water from A to B using basic materials like dowels, guttering and elastic bands. They were then assessed on how quickly they transferred the water and how much of it survived the journey!

Case study – London pupils' rapid response to disaster in 2005

Fulham was struck by a theoretical hurricane, as the Rapid Response Engineering Challenge got under way at Imperial Wharf.

The event, in which 60 local pupils responded to a natural disaster scenario, was organised by the Construction Industry Training Board (CITB) Construction Skills in partnership with local secondary schools, Hammersmith & Fulham Council's education business section and Imperial Wharf developer St George.

Teams of 13–14-year-old pupils from Fulham Cross, Hurlingham and Chelsea, Burlington Danes and Henry Compton secondary schools competed to build emergency shelters and a water system in response to a Hurricane Mitch-style natural disaster, demonstrating the key role civil engineering has in such dire emergencies.

Beginning in a marquee at Imperial Wharf, the day comprised indoor and outdoor activities – including presentations, role-play and group work. The pupils were divided into teams and asked to consider a range of logistical problems, including flooding risks, fuel sources, health hazards and environmental impact. They then built their emergency shelters and water systems.

Michael Meanley, Managing Director of St George Central London commented: 'We hope the pupils will discover engineering to be a challenging, varied and adventurous discipline.'

Cllr Melanie Smallman, Hammersmith & Fulham Council's cabinet member for education, said: 'This challenging exercise for local secondary school pupils provided an exciting way for young people from local schools to work together and develop their problem solving, presentation and practical skills. We have many successful partnerships with organisations that are giving young people a wide range of work-related experiences.'

BA CREST Awards

BA CREST is a nationally recognised accreditation scheme for project work in the fields of science and technology. Aimed at students aged 11–19, BA CREST awards encourage students to develop their curiosity, problem solving and communication skills.

Through a mentoring system, the scheme facilitates links between schools and industry or higher education. It enables students of all abilities to explore real scientific, engineering and technological problems for themselves and promotes work-related learning.

BA CREST awards motivate students, build confidence and encourage them to pursue careers in science, engineering and technology.

BA CREST awards are available in **Technology** – at three levels:

Bronze:

- ten hours of project work
- typically for ages 11–14.

Silver:

- 40 hours of project work
- typically for students aged 14–16
- links with industry encouraged.

Gold:

- 100 hours of project work

- typically for students aged 16+

- students linked with a mentor from industry or higher education

- can accredit Nuffield Bursary placements and Engineering Education Scheme (EES) project work.

Students who have completed BA CREST project work have the opportunity to display their work at Regional Finals. Outstanding projects are selected for the prestigious national BA CREST Science Fair (www.the-ba.net/the-ba/ ResourcesforLearning/BACRESTScienceFair/).

Technology projects should similarly be assessed, by asking whether students have successfully:

- described the need or problem they want to solve

- written a clear design brief for what they intended to do

- researched background information and produced an outline specification

- generated and developed as many ideas as they can to solve the need or problem (minimum of two)

- evaluated their ideas, giving reasons why they chose or rejected them

- developed a chosen idea using clear notes and diagrams to illustrate the proposed solution

- produced a step-by-step plan for manufacture

- listed all the tools and materials that they intended to use

- manufactured their chosen design

- evaluated the finished product in relation to the original design brief and specification

- communicated their knowledge and enthusiasm.

Working with a mentor

A mentor is someone from outside the school who has expertise relevant to the project. For example, it might be someone from a local company, or someone who works in higher or further education. Mentors are usually found through local or regional SETPOINTs, the Science and Engineering Ambassadors Scheme (SEAS) or the Researchers in Residence (RiR) scheme. Mentors usually become involved by talking to students about the context of their work. They might:

- act as an 'expert witness', providing information and/or resources

- be a point of access for specialist equipment or techniques

- provide relevant work experience or arrange an industrial visit

- help students develop their ideas and guide them as they look at their results

- provide a different perspective to a problem.

Mentors shouldn't tell students what to do, but help them develop the project as far as possible.

At gold level, project mentors are compulsory. The mentor should meet regularly with the student(s) during the project to discuss progress. Mentors should also be involved with the final evaluation of the project.

Example projects

Jeans

www.the-ba.net/the-ba/ResourcesforLearning/ BACRESTAwards/ProjectIdeas/Fashion/ Clothing/

'I wear jeans all the time . . . I have . . . all kinds of jeans. I love jeans'. Gwyneth Paltrow is a big jeans fan. Jeans are a must-have fashion accessory. They've changed style many times over the years, but have always bounced back. Not bad going for a piece of clothing originally designed to keep miners clean in the US about 150 years ago.

Have you ever wondered why some jeans are a lot more expensive than others? Are designer jeans any tougher than cheap jeans?
You might like to . . .

- carry out tests to compare the resistance to wear and tear of denim from expensive jeans and from cheap jeans
- compare the strength of the seams on different types of jeans (for example, look at different types of seam, thread and sewing patterns).

Spuds

www.the-ba.net/the-ba/ ResourcesforLearning/ BACRESTAwards/ProjectIdeas/FoodandDrink/ CrispsandSpuds/Spuds.htm

When buying a packet of crisps, an interesting colour isn't usually one of the things we actively seek. The golden brown variety is just fine, thanks. But if you did fancy something

different, there's a Staffordshire food company that make blue crisps. They're made from a blue variety of Scandinavian potato, which means no artificial colourings have to be added. They're blue-ming marvellous, apparently.

Have you ever wondered why some varieties of potato are used to make crisps whereas others are used for chip making, baking, boiling and mashing?
You might like to . . .

- find out how to make crisps
- choose different brands of potato and compare their suitability for crisp production. See if varieties of white potato are better for crisp production than red varieties, for example
- find out what happens to crisps when new potatoes are used to make them
- investigate the effect of adding a coating to crisps.

Further information:

www.esa.org.uk/education/english

Electronic devices

www.the-ba.net/the-ba/ResourcesforLearning/BACRESTAwards/ProjectIdeas/
Entertainment/RobotsGames/Electronicdevices.htm

Electronic devices are all around us! Electric circuits control millions of everyday objects. And the electronic circuitry seems to be getting smaller and smaller. Mobile phones are a good example; if they get any smaller they'd slip through the fibres of your jeans! Then there are walkmans, mini-disc players, palm-tops and calculators. Even a lot of car keys these days have a small electric circuit so you can 'bleep' and open the door. Are we becoming that lazy?

Have you ever wondered how to make your own electronic device?
You might like to . . .
- find out about electronic devices (you'll need to know about power supplies, input devices, processors and output devices)
- decide on a use for your electronic device (some examples are: rain alarm, automatic night light, strain gauge)
- design and make your electronic device (you'll have to find out about techniques such as soldering or making printed circuit boards. You'll also have to think about how to shape, cut and join materials to make a case to house your device)
- think about how your device could be mass-produced.

Note: The level of this project can increase by introducing more variables and more complex electrical circuitry; the things an electronic device can do are almost limitless!

Born to skate

www.the-ba.net/the-ba/ResourcesforLearning/BACRESTAwards/ProjectIdeas/
Sport/ExtremeSports

A friend of mine recently took his skateboard to ride a bowl at his local skate park. Within minutes the other boarders heard a crunch; they turned round to see my mate poleaxed on the ground with a somewhat contorted wrist displaying his bones in an unnatural way. At hospital his legs had to be held down as the wrist was snapped back into place before being put in a plaster cast. The shots of morphine didn't kill the pain, but he still went boarding the next day. Skaters . . . they're crazy aren't they?

Have you ever wondered what skateboards are made from? And how the design helps skaters pull tricks?
You might like to . . .

- find out about skateboard design; find out how it's changed over the years; find out why some boards are 'concave'; find out why the noses turn up
- find out what materials are used to make the board; design and carry out tests on different materials to see which would be suitable for making a skateboard
- find out how the wheels are made, and what they're made from; find out how this has changed over the years
- design and carry out tests on different skateboard wheels; decide which properties you think are required first
- find out how trucks are made and what they do; test different trucks
- design and make a skateboard (or a single component); test your board (or component)
- design and make a skateboard ramp; think about the materials you'd need.

Further information:
www.exploratorium.edu/skateboarding/

Ride the waves

www.the-ba.net/the-ba/ResourcesforLearning/BACRESTAwards/ProjectIdeas/
Sport/ExtremeSports/Ridethewaves.htm

Pro-surfers make a fair few pounds (or, more likely, dollars) for their wave-carving antics. And it's not a bad lifestyle; the likes of Taj Burrows, Kelly Slater and Rob Machardo spend their days on the ASP World Tour, jet-setting round the globe, ripping waves to pieces in places like Fiji, Hawaii and Indonesia. All they need is a board and a block of wax.

Have you ever wondered how surfboards are designed and made? And why do surfers wax their sticks?

You might like to . . .

- find out about surfboard design and manufacture; find out how designs and techniques have changed over the years; find out the difference between 'pop-out' boards and 'custom' boards; find out what makes them strong/ waterproof
- investigate the effect of using different shapes for surfboards; find out how they're designed to stop them flipping over on the water; find out how long boards and short boards react differently in the waves
- investigate the effects of using different size/shape/number of fins
- find out why surfers wax their boards; carry out tests to investigate the effectiveness of different surf wax; try to make your own wax
- link up with some professional surfboard designers and design and make your own board
- investigate what creates waves; try to make a wave machine that creates breaking waves (not a ripple tank).

Further information:

www.noisenet.ws/sports/index.htm

www.the-ba.net/the-ba/ResourcesforLearning/BACRESTAwards/

The Arkwright Scholarship Scheme

www.arkwright.org.uk/index.html

This scheme encourages a partnership to promote design and technology leading to careers in engineering.

Student requirements

To be considered for an Arkwright Scholarship a student should be:

- considering higher education in engineering, product or industrial design

- in Year 11 (final year of GCSE or Scottish Standard Grades)

- making a commitment to D&T at AS level and preferably to A2 in the sixth form or alternatively able to demonstrate enthusiasm and aptitude in practical engineering or technology

- making a commitment to mathematics at AS Level and preferably to A2 in the sixth form.

Up to 15 Scholarships per annum will be available for outstanding candidates who do not intend to take mathematics beyond GCSE level. Candidates sit the Arkwright Aptitude Paper designed to encourage the individuals to demonstrate their skills by producing innovative solutions to problems.

School requirements

To be considered for membership of the Arkwright Scholarship Scheme, schools:

- should have Year 11 (Scottish Standard Grade) students studying design and technology/technological studies in Scotland (hereon referred to as D&T) or have feeder schools offering the subject

- should be teaching D&T or engineering-related subjects at A2 (Highers in Scotland) or equivalent

- should have a headteacher who is a strong supporter of D&T in the curriculum

- should present opportunities to participate in related activities outside the curriculum.

Benefits

- The scholar will receive £500 over two years and the school's D&T department will receive £450 split over the two years

- Public recognition of the excellence of D&T in the school

- Opportunity to work with business and industry

- Raises the profile of the subject with younger people

- Provides a springboard to interact with other centres of excellence at high profile events

- Exposes capable students to the experience of scholarship assessment

- Scholars are matched to a sponsor by regional location and/or career aspirations

- Receive details of opportunities, relating to career aspirations, such as engineering awareness courses, company open days

- Opportunities to network with other scholars through the Arkwright Alumni (to be introduced)

- Scholars may approach their sponsor for work experience and/or careers advice

- Possible sponsorship from sponsors while studying at university or work in the vacations.

THE IKB Awards – Engineering Award 14–18 years

www.brunel.ac.uk/ikbawards

The awards scheme asks students to think about the problems that face the world today – and how engineers could help to tackle them. For example:

- crime

- disease and illness

- global warming

- natural disasters – earthquakes, volcanoes and tidal waves

- pollution

- terrorism

- developing world poverty.

They are asked to think about:

- **People:** Who will benefit from their solution? What will they use it for? Will they find it useful?

- **Technology:** What technology will their solution use and how will it work?

- **Society:** Why will others think it is a good idea?

- **The Market:** How they will market your solution?

CHAPTER 7

Beyond the classroom

> Finding a gifted designer is a wonderful experience – but being gifted doesn't necessarily mean being successful – and whilst some brilliant designers wouldn't give a fig for commercial success, for others, hard work and sheer determination will overcome all hurdles that life puts between them and their goals.
>
> (Claire Curtis-Thomas MP)

There are many opportunities to provide for more able pupils beyond schools and particularly classrooms. Many pupils benefit from design and technology specialist summer schools, an activity week, work experience, after-school clubs, masterclasses and 24-hour Challenges.

Questions for an INSET activity

- Review school, local or national competitions that pupils can be encouraged to enter
- Consider how these might be used: school clubs, masterclasses, suspended timetable weeks.

Case study – an activity week or day for able pupils

Activity Week QCA Unit 7E

Based on the model of using a suspended timetable for one day (shown in QCA/DfEE scheme of work) Hassenbrook School developed a programme called Mission Impossible for 24 Year 8 pupils who had been identified with special abilities in maths, D&T and English. Pupils worked in groups and a presentation at the start of the day gave them a clear focus. Their mission was to:

- form a company with an appropriate name and logo
- explain the importance of sustainable development

- design a product to meet the requirements of the situation
- design and make packaging for the product
- produce an A4 sheet on their product
- make a group presentation at the end of the day to the head and the local environmental officer and the School's environmental group organiser.

All the information for the day had to be accessed through computers in the library and ICT suite. Two teachers were available for consultation and guidance.

The topic of sustainability, and the pace and group skills demanded by the scale of the tasks presented a challenging day for the group.

Gain as much experience as possible. This may mean working for free. The design industry is and always has been an oversubscribed career path to take. You will have to work hard and produce a high quality body of work if you are to stand out from the crowd. Originality, self-belief and determination should see you through.

(Donna Fullman, Design Director of Eyefood, www.eyefood.net)

Case study – masterclasses

Young Enterprise Entrepreneurship Masterclasses

www.young-enterprise.org.uk/programmes/em.asp

www.yeherts.org.uk

Releasing the entrepreneurial flair and potential of our young people is a key objective for Young Enterprise. The Entrepreneurship Masterclass is a one/half-day seminar that challenges students to think about starting their own business as a career, and becoming an entrepreneur, through enabling today's entrepreneurs to inspire those of tomorrow. This is achieved by introducing the students to real entrepreneurs who share their vision, experiences and achievements.

The Entrepreneurship Masterclass offers an exciting programme designed to meet the needs of our future entrepreneurs. The day includes fun and interactive workshop sessions to help students think about and rehearse responses to the themes, ideas and obstacles associated with entrepreneurship. In addition there are presentation elements to the day from local entrepreneurs, during which students have the opportunity to ask questions and seek advice.

Through participating in an Entrepreneurship Masterclass students gain:

- an understanding from experts of what is involved in setting up their own business
- knowledge of the technical process of setting up a business from the experience of others who have become today's entrepreneurs
- an understanding of the need of related experiences before becoming tomorrow's entrepreneurs
- inspiration, enthusiasm and vision.

Case study – suspend the timetable

24-hour challenge

36 D&T A Level students and their teachers from 12 Welsh schools took part in an event arranged by the University of Wales Institute Cardiff. This intensive weekend gave the students and teachers the opportunity to work in teams on a brief that explored the development of a new sport or game. The emphasis was on creativity, techniques for generating ideas and skills associated with working in teams and presenting ideas. All had a wonderful if tiring weekend and those running the event were impressed by the quality of many of the ideas the groups came up with. The AUDI Foundation who part-sponsored this pilot event are considering further similar events elsewhere in the UK, and also the production of associated resource materials to support teachers in schools and colleges.

Case study – after-school clubs

After-school clubs

www.youngeng.org

Young Engineers runs over 1,583 Young Engineers' Clubs nationwide for young people aged 7–19. At the present time they have over 13,000 members, with the gap between girls and boys getter smaller: approximately 40% girls, 60% boys. Young Engineers' Clubs promote the importance of engineering in a practical way, but also offer young people the opportunity to take part in design-and-make projects, compete in regional and national competitions, visit companies and work with professional engineers.

Case study – community programmes

EC1 Young Engineers Challenge

www.city.ac.uk/careers/cv/projects/ec1/engineering.html

The EC1 Young Engineers Challenge is one of the City's groundbreaking community focused programmes that develop new skills and raise the aspirations of young people in the local community. It is part of the EC1 – 3 Way Street Project. City Racing Team Manager, Roger Valsler, has developed an exceptional programme that brings engineering theory to life for 14-year-olds. It is designed to encourage gifted and talented pupils from local schools to stay in post-16 education. The project actively addresses many of the perceived barriers to entry or negative preconceptions they may have had about higher education and engineering in particular.

In 2005 they were piloting this project through local schools and it is hoped to broaden access to this project in the future.

The project aims to enable young people to:

- become an expert in karting
- be a part of the first EC1 Racing Team

- visit the International Formula Student competition in Nottingham
- get expert advice on careers and opportunities in engineering
- speak up for young people in EC1.

Participants take part in 14 sessions including:

- eight 'Practical engineering' sessions where they will learn about how to use the tools, chassis theory, engines, drive, steering, wheels and tyres, driving techniques, etc.
- three 'Make it better' sessions where they will take part in working with adults to improve provision for residents in EC1. These sessions are run by the Islington Youth Offending Service
- two 'Day trips' including a visit to the International Formula Student competition, which this year will be held in Leicester and a day at the track to test their kart before it is taken apart for rebuilding.

Far from being a gentle introduction to engineering, this programme was designed to challenge the young people and make them think and act as a team. So far they have attended a series of lectures on topics including an introduction to tyre and chassis technology, the theory of braking systems, steering dynamics and wind tunnel applications. In addition they have dismantled and rebuilt their own high-performance karts, visited the Formula Student Competition in support of the City University team, brought a kart they built to the track for testing, piloted City University's flight simulator and appeared in the Lord Mayor's Show in November.

Now they have returned to school they are receiving continued support from across the University to help them manage their own after-school karting project. They have access to careers advice and workshops from the Centre for Career and Skills Development, student experience from volunteer student mentors who work alongside them.

Industry experts such as Roger and his colleagues in the School of Engineering and Mathematical Sciences are helping them with any technical problems they have.

Case studies – work-related learning

Work experience and working with companies outside school

Pupils from specialist schools in four London boroughs took part in a project studying architecture and design as part of a project managed by Crossrail.

The scheme, which is part of the company's Young Crossrail activity programme, is run in association with London Gifted and Talented, the Specialist Schools Trust and the Canary Wharf Group.

Students work with designers, architects and engineers for ten weeks to develop a design brief for a new Crossrail station at Canary Wharf, an essential part of the Crossrail route.

The Canary Wharf Group commented: 'Crossrail is all about the future growth and development of London, and from what we have seen so far we are sure many of these students will be playing a significant role as the next generation of talented Londoners.'

Ian Warwick, London Gifted & Talented's Development Director, commented: 'This course is based firmly in a real world situation with challenge and innovation at the core. It is a chance to highlight how a gifted student can be involved with a vocational course.'

Barry McGregor, subject leader for engineering colleges, at the Specialist Schools Trust, said: 'This is an excellent opportunity for students to be involved in a real engineering project. The project aims to demonstrate that 'engineering' is innovative, exciting and rewarding, and that it impacts on all aspects of our lives. The work produced is an exciting way in which to promote engineering in its many forms.'

Whilst I fully appreciate the level of work involved in being a teacher I believe it is essential to ensure all design teachers are aware of the current design climate. Things have changed enormously since I studied design and yet the teaching styles and awareness remains very similar to those of some 15 years ago. The design and technology world moves at an increasing pace and is a job in itself to keep up. However, it is essential to remain interested and involved at teacher level to inspire and encourage interest in pupils. In simple terms: Teachers need to be aware and excited by the industries in order to inspire students.

(Donna Fullman, Design Director of Eyefood, www.eyefood.net)

Manufacturing links with local industry

John Port School in South Derbyshire has developed a partnership with Toyota Motor Manufacturing, UK, Ltd. Each week two engineers from Toyota come to the school to raise the profile of both engineering and manufacturing. They provide real-life insights and 'hands-on' activities, sometimes with the latest technology and innovations.

Together, they have set the projects for the pupils. For example, the engineers described a current problem they have and asked the pupils to come up with solutions.

The problem

Soundproof asphalt sheets are placed into the cars and baked in an oven as part of the paint hardening process. Dust created from these sheets often gets on to visible paintwork and has to be removed and treated, creating an 'on-cost' to the manufacturer.

Brief

To research, design and manufacture a prototype system to prevent dust particles from asphalt soundproofing sheets damaging the paintwork of Toyota car body shells during the assembly process.

What the pupils did

The pupils visited the factory to meet with engineers and to get an insight into the size and range of activities. Pupils were asked to identify a range of areas where they could see potential problems/areas for improvement. They ended the visit with a brainstorming session and choosing tasks.

For the nest few weeks, the engineers, teachers and students met at the school, where an analysis of the problem was made. The students were asked to brainstorm a range of possible methods to prevent particles of dust from breaking off the asphalt sheets. Two solutions appeared to be favourites:

1. Heating the asphalt would ensure it was pliable and not brittle.
2. Spraying a fine mist of water would ensure the dust particles were damped down.

After comprehensive testing of both proposals, the production of a fine mist spray was agreed.

On a second visit the pupils assessed ways of getting a spray into the cars whilst the cars were moving on a conveyor belt system. They took detailed measurements and timings for the particular section of the production line. They split the work into three groups:

1. Make a scale model of the conveyor belt system.
2. Investigate mechanisms for creating a pneumatic arm to enter the cars through the front window aperture to deliver the mist spray.
3. Develop a control programme to operate the conveyor belt and the pneumatic arm.

The pupils produced a series of prototypes of the system. This involved engineering skills in the development and production of the components for the conveyor belt model and pneumatic arm, construction skills with the design of the scale model; ICT skills with the development of the 'Logicator' programme, CAD skills designing all components using Pro Desktop; and throughout the process a great deal of problem solving skills.

The pupils also developed graphic skills, both using CAD and manual applications, and developed both their communication skills and confidence throughout.

After modelling and development they made a presentation to directors and senior managers and the engineers have now developed the concept.

This problem was both demanding and exacting. The benefit of this project for more able pupils is that they see their ideas put into practice in real situations, they evaluate and analyse real-life working practice, they experience innovative technology, and work in a team situation as equals with adult helpers/facilitators.

Case studies – G&T day programmes and residential courses

At-Bristol's gifted and talented day programmes

In July–August each year www.at-bristol.org.uk run a series of day programmes; they are now in their fourth year.

Each day includes some of the following:

- practical investigations
- team activities
- working with role models from universities, industry or government
- discussing and debating, for example, exploring the social and ethical implications of science and technology
- a team challenge in an interactive exhibition such as Explore or Wildwalk
- use of NewMediaLab and TV Studio
- work-related learning
- careers information
- follow-up activities on the At-Bristol website Environment Days.

Biodiversity and sustainable development

At-Bristol's G &T Environment days provide Key Stage 3 students with an opportunity to take a closer look at our planet, its variety of ecosystems and the effect of human actions on them. Integrating sections of the D&T, Biology, Geography and Citizenship curriculum, students will have the chance to visit the tropical rainforest gallery and contribute to the content of the People and Planet exhibition redevelopment.

Earthquake Engineering Challenge

Run in association with the Department of Civil Engineering, University of Bristol, the Earthquake Engineering Challenge will be to work in a team to design and construct a model of a building to a scale of roughly 1:25. The model should stand up to the artificial earthquakes generated on the shaking-table in the University of Bristol's Earthquake Engineering Research Centre's laboratory, and can be constructed only from MDF board, paper, string and glue. They also have the opportunity to visit the exhibitions in Explore At-Bristol.

Kingswood's gifted and talented residential courses

Kingswood's range of courses for more able students recognise the varying needs within any specific group. Their programmes are designed so that Gifted and Talented pupils learn at different speeds and also develop leadership, decision-making and organisational skills. 'Gifted and talented' students may demonstrate high academic, sporting or artistic ability; however, gifted learners may have abilities in one or more academic subjects such as maths and English, and talented learners may display abilities in sport, music, design or creative and performing arts.

For the last five years Kingswood has been working with the DfES and regional initiatives as well as gifted and talented coordinators in supporting gifted and talented pupils, particularly in urban areas. A visit to Kingswood forms part of the schools' individual teaching and learning programmes, and extra study support for their gifted and talented pupils.

The gifted and talented courses are 'real-life' scenarios that involve students in group activities with teamwork and team building as core elements of a full key skill programme. The courses have been designed by education specialists in conjunction with the Excellence in Cities programme, and meet the criteria laid down by the DfES for developing gifted young people. The Lifeskills Academy combines personal development with teambuilding and key skill development.

Example – Self-parking car

Using the latest Lego Dacta Robolab technology, the task is to design, build and market an 'intelligent' vehicle. This is the cutting edge of control technology! The design requires students to analyse market research data and assess their market. Working to tight budgets, students will need not only to map their inventory requirements, but also refine their programming skills. This is a team task that concludes when the young inventors create a showcase presentation for their target audience.

www.kingswood.co.uk/pages/courses_gifted.html

The Smallpeice Trust's engineering residential courses

Smallpeice www.smallpeicetrust.org.uk

The Smallpeice Trust run residential courses to promote engineering as a career to young people from the age of 13 to 18.

The Engineering Experience

The residential courses begin at Year 9. The engineering experience is designed to introduce the broad areas of this subject to students who are considering their GCSE options. During the residential, students have access to materials and equipments that may not be available to them in school. This is a unique opportunity for them to build on the knowledge gained in lessons. This is applied during the design and make projects and workshops, which are based on real-life scenarios. Professionals are on hand to offer advice and guidance both on the project and engineering as a potential career.

One of the most valuable elements of the course for many students is the teambuilding activities, which focus on developing interpersonal skills that are needed to be successful both in the challenge and in the future. It is a four-day residential course designed specifically to help students reach design and technology Level 6 and higher attainment target of the National Curriculum.

It aims to improve technical ability, develop new skills and increase knowledge through:

- product analysis
- design and make assignments, involving control systems and using a range of contrasting materials
- practical application of techniques and processes
- working within budgets and calculate the financial implications of decisions
- innovation and entrepreneurship.

Students have the opportunity to learn about work practices alongside young engineers chosen from a range of industries, working on projects that are based on their real-life challenges. Throughout the course they will guide students through all the development stages, from concept to final testing and presentation of their project.

The key skills that the project activities are designed to develop include:

- communication and presentation skills
- improving learning and performance
- information technology
- problem solving and creativity
- teamworking and leadership
- numeracy and analysis.

The creative thinking and analytical skills to:

- collect relevant information for their project and analyse it
- make reasoned judgements and look for alternative outcomes
- plan what to do, test and improve ideas
- evaluate and judge their own and the team's designs
- devise an interesting business presentation of their final design.

Certificate of achievement

On successful completion of the course to the required standard, students are presented with a certificate of achievement, a valuable addition to their record of achievement.

What do pupils get out of residential courses such as Smallpeice?

(by David Dunn, head of design and technology at Yarm School)

As any head of department will testify, there are a good number of organisations that now aim to support the teaching of Design and Technology. Some offer competitions while others prepare teaching materials. All this is good news, in that opportunities are created for pupils – opportunities that stimulate imagination and help harness enthusiasm for the world of engineering and design.

Like me, you may also feel that there are signs of resurgence in the belief that there is significant value for children in the 'Knowing How' in addition to the 'Knowing That'. In other words, the application of understanding can lead to adding value in any number of ways. 'Knowing How' is delivered not only through quality curriculum experiences, but also from encouraging and challenging children. Capturing interest is the key and opportunities are there for the taking.

Each year I encourage pupils to apply for the residential courses run by The Smallpeice Trust. Not only are they excellent value for money and exemplary in terms of the experience they offer, but more importantly they 'capture interest', an interest in the exciting world that a career in engineering can offer. The desirable qualities of confidence, self-belief and independence of mind are nurtured, and they are truly valuable.

As teachers, we all see in pupils those who have an affinity with 'the made world' – pupils who work materials with great interest and simply want to 'Know-How' and also 'Know That'. For a 14-year-old it is a big step to attend a residential course. Encouragement and support can lead to real rewards.

Energy Challenge

(by Nicola Turner, Monkwearmouth School, Sunderland)

I'd decided to come on the course as I was interested in engineering. It proved to be an extreme eye-opener....

The first thing on the agenda was to get everyone into their groups, and to 'break the ice'. We spent the morning coming up with a team name that would do our final design proud – TANAG, the first letter of everyone's name.

That afternoon there was the first competition of the day – 'Design and build a jet powered car'. Spirits high, TANAG threw themselves into the project. Drawing on everyone's expertise, we became a crack team of engineers, as the time came to test our cars. First car, no movement, we celebrated. Second car, third, fourth and fifth, the same again. Our turn. TANAG's winged monster flew from the starting line like the proverbial bullet from a gun, then came to a sorry stop, its wheels all rolling in different directions around the room. We'd done it! Not only won the project, but created a reputation for ourselves. Victory was sweet.

The next day we split up, went to the workshop in which we would slave for the next couple of days, and go to choose our expert. Stacy – ours – was a great help, as she made constructive criticism and basically became a key member of TANAG. As the team designer, I came up with loads of drawings that the team picked holes in and discarded until we came up with an original design. It really was a challenge – Stacy, with her experience could point out some potential problems, and work with us to come up with a solution. Without our expert, team TANAG's radical new windmill would never have come to fruition. We got two days to work on our windmill, and at the end there was a panicked rush to make sure all of the features worked. We had to overcome more than a few problems, but we managed to do this using teamwork, and at the end of the making time, we were happy with our final project.

We took our windmill to the wind tunnel to test it. The wind was turned on – for a few tense moments the windmill did not rotate. Then, it started to revolve, slowly gathering speed and momentum. YES! Our turbine produced about 3.6 volts, amazing, bringing us in at second place.

In between making our wind turbine, our hectic schedule was filled with things like going to the Shell company office. That was a great experience – getting an insight into how real marine engineers and technicians work.

I would definitely, without a doubt, recommend a Smallpeice event to anyone. I learnt about engineering and so much more, and would now consider a career in the field. It was a challenge (as the name suggests!) as you were constantly pushed to evolve your ideas further, to make them the best they could be.

Other case studies can be found on the accompanying CD.

Appendices

Ofsted – Expectations of schools in relation to able pupils

Evaluation focus	Issue	Judgement/evidence
Effectiveness of school	Inclusion/equal opportunities	• High achievement is determined by 'the school's commitment to inclusion and the steps it takes to ensure that *every* pupil does as well as possible.' (p. 25) • At the parents' meeting, inspectors should find out if, in the view of parents, 'their children are progressing as well as they could; their children are happy in school, well taught and well cared for; the extent to which the school promotes equality of opportunity between different groups and includes *all* pupils and parents.' (p. 38)
Standards achieved by pupils	Achievement and underachievement	• Inspectors are asked to look at the achievement of different groups. (p. 44) • 'If they (pupils) are readily capable of work beyond that which they are doing, they are underachieving.' (p. 45) • A school should know 'how well gifted and talented pupils do and, where appropriate, how well pupils do in the school's specialist subjects ... Inspectors should judge how well the school uses information to identify and deal with underachievement, challenge the most capable and raise standards for all pupils.' (p. 48)
	Early entry	• Inspectors should be aware of special circumstances, such as 'a school policy on early entry for GCSE for some pupils.' • 'Where pupils are entered early for GCSE examinations, inspectors should take account of the results in reaching a judgement about the performance of the year group as a whole and consider what early entry has allowed the pupils to achieve subsequently.' (p. 47)
	Discussion with pupils	• Inspectors should 'talk to pupils of different ages and levels of attainment (including) ... the high achievers.' (p. 54)
	Assessment	• Assessment might guide planning through 'review of pupils' progress, including whether targets have been met at the end of a unit of work to inform teaching and target-setting for the whole class, groups and individuals.' (p. 88) • Inspectors should observe 'how targets for individual pupils of all abilities are agreed ...' (p. 88) • Inspectors should take samples of students' work to see 'how assessment contributes to planning work for gifted and talented pupils ... and how the outcomes are considered in reviews.' (p. 88)

 From *Meeting the Needs of Your Most Able Pupils: Design and Technology*, David Fulton Publishers 2006

Evaluation focus	Issue	Judgement/evidence
Quality of education	Teachers' command of subject	● 'Pupils should be learning from experts.' ● 'Teachers' knowledge is demonstrated in the way they . . . cater for the more able in a subject.' (p. 77)
	Appropriate challenge	● 'Effective teaching extends pupils intellectually, creatively and physically. Inspectors should judge whether teachers are determined to get the best out of the pupils and if they are being challenged enough.' (p. 78) ● Inspectors are advised to 'observe what is done to challenge the most able pupils in the class, including those who may be identified by the school as gifted and talented. Watch for those pupils who are clearly not being challenged enough. What is the effect of lack of challenge on them? Where no obvious special provision is being made, find out why.' (p. 81)
	Learning methods and resources	● Judge the approaches used for pupils of high ability.' (p. 79) ● Inspectors should assess whether 'teachers involve all pupils in lessons, giving the diffident and the slower learners a chance to contribute and time to answer questions, and yet challenging the most able.' (p. 75)
	Homework	● 'How well is homework tailored to individual needs and capabilities?' (p. 81)
	Equality of access (to the curriculum)	● 'Does it take account of their cultural background and religious beliefs, diverse ethnic backgrounds, special educational needs and particular gifts or talents?' (p. 100)
	Pupil care	● Evidence of the care of pupils will include provision for those who are gifted and talented. (p. 109)
Management	Inclusion	● Does the school provide successfully for pupils who . . . are gifted and talented?' (p. 144)
Schools causing concern	Underachieving schools	● 'Triggers that might suggest a school is underachieving include: . . . lack of challenge and slow progress for particular groups of pupils (for example the most able), in certain classes, a particular stage or in several subjects.' (p. 164)
Initiatives for raising achievement	Excellence in Cities	● 'Gifted and Talented pupils should be identified in EiC schools . . . The school should have a policy and teaching programme for these pupils. Inspectors should evaluate the effectiveness of the school's strategy in motivating gifted and talented pupils and ensuring that they achieve as well as they can both in lessons and extracurricular activities.' (p. 30)

The page numbers refer to the Ofsted *Handbook for Inspecting Secondary Schools* (2003).

 From *Meeting the Needs of Your Most Able Pupils: Design and Technology*, David Fulton Publishers 2006

National quality standards in gifted and talented education

A – Effective teaching and learning strategies

Generic Elements	Entry	Developing	Exemplary
1. Identification	i. The school/college has learning conditions and systems to identify gifted and talented pupils in all year groups and an agreed definition and shared understanding of the meaning of 'gifted and talented' within its own, local and national contexts	i. Individual pupils are screened annually against clear criteria at school/college and subject/topic level	i. **Multiple criteria and sources of evidence** are used to identify gifts and talents, including through the use of a broad range of quantitative and qualitative data
	ii. An **accurate record** of the identified gifted and talented population is kept and updated.	ii. The record is used to identify under-achievement and **exceptional achievement** (both within and outside the population) and to track/review pupil progress	ii. The record is supported by a comprehensive monitoring, progress planning and reporting system which all staff regularly share and contribute to
	iii. The identified gifted and talented population broadly reflects the school/college's **social and economic composition, gender and ethnicity**	iii. Identification systems address issues of **multiple exceptionality** (pupils with specific gifts/talents and special educational needs)	iii. **Identification** processes are regularly reviewed and refreshed in the light of pupil performance and value-added data. The gifted and talented population is fully repre-sentative of the school/college's population
Evidence			
Next steps			
2. Effective provision in the classroom	i. The school/college addresses the different needs of the gifted and talented population by providing a stimulating learning environment and by extending the teaching repertoire	i. Teaching and learning strategies are diverse and flexible, meeting the needs of distinct pupil groups within the gifted and talented population (e.g. able underachievers, exceptionally able)	i. The school/college has established a range of methods to find out what works best in the classroom, and shares this within the school/college and with other schools and colleges
	ii. Teaching and learning is differentiated and delivered through both individual and group activities	ii. A range of challenging learning and teaching strategies is evident in lesson planning and delivery. **Independent** learning skills are developed.	ii. Teaching and learning are suitably challenging and varied, incorporating the **breadth, depth and pace** required to progress high achievement. Pupils routinely work independently and self-reliantly

	Entry	Developing	Exemplary
	iii. Opportunities exist to extend learning through **new technologies**	iii. The use of **new technologies** across the curriculum is focused on **personalised learning** needs	iii. The innovative use of **new technologies** raises the achievement and motivation of gifted and talented pupils
Evidence			
Next steps			
3. Standards	i. Levels of **attainment** and **achievement** for gifted and talented pupils are comparatively high in relation to the rest of the school/college population and are in line with those of similar pupils in similar schools/colleges	i. Levels of **attainment** and **achievement** for gifted and talented pupils are broadly consistent across the gifted and talented population and above those of similar pupils in similar schools/colleges	i. Levels of **attainment** and **achievement** for gifted and talented pupils indicate sustainability over time and are well above those of similar pupils in similar schools/colleges
	ii. Self-evaluation indicates that gifted and talented provision is satisfactory	ii. Self-evaluation indicates that gifted and talented provision is good	ii. Self-evaluation indicates that gifted and talented provision is very good or excellent
	iii. Schools/colleges gifted and talented education programmes are explicitly linked to the achievement of SMART outcomes and these highlight improvements in pupils' attainment and achievement		
Evidence			
Next steps			

B – Enabling curriculum entitlement and choice

	Entry	Developing	Exemplary
4. Enabling curriculum entitlement and choice	i. Curriculum organisation is flexible, with opportunities for enrichment and increasing subject/topic choice. Pupils are provided with support and guidance in making choices	i. The curriculum offers opportunities and guidance to pupils which enable them to work beyond their age and/or phase, and across subjects or topics, according to their aptitudes and interests	i. The curriculum offers **personalised learning pathways** for pupils which maximise individual potential, retain flexibility of future choices, extend well beyond test/examination requirements and result in sustained impact on pupil attainment and achievement
Evidence			
Next steps			

Definitions for words and phrases in bold are provided in the glossary in the Quality Standards *User Guide*, available at www2.teachernet.gov.uk/gat.
© Crown copyright 2005

Generic Elements	Entry	Developing	Exemplary
C – Assessment for learning			
5. Assessment for learning	i. Processes of data analysis and pupil assessment are employed throughout the school/college to plan learning for gifted and talented pupils	i. Routine progress reviews, using both qualitative and quantitative data, make effective use of prior, predictive and value-added **attainment** data to plan for progression in pupils' learning	i. **Assessment data** are used by teachers and across the school/college to ensure challenge and sustained progression in individual pupils' learning
	ii. Dialogue with pupils provides focused feedback which is used to plan future learning	ii. Systematic oral and written feedback helps pupils to set challenging curricular targets	ii. Formative assessment and individual target-setting combine to maximise and celebrate pupils' achievements
	iii. Self and peer assessment, based on clear understanding of criteria, are used to increase pupils' responsibility for learning	iii. Pupils reflect on their own skill development and are involved in the design of their own targets and tasks	iii. Classroom practice regularly requires pupils to reflect on their own **progress** against targets, and engage in the direction of their own learning
Evidence			
Next steps			
6. Transfer and transition	i. Shared processes, using agreed criteria, are in place to ensure the productive transfer of information from one setting to another (i.e. from class to class, year to year and school/college to school/college)	i. Transfer information concerning gifted and talented pupils, including parental input, informs targets for pupils to ensure **progress** in learning. Particular attention is given to including new admissions	i. Transfer data concerning gifted and talented pupils are used to inform planning of teaching and learning at subject/aspect/topic and individual pupil level, and to ensure progression according to ability rather than age or phase
Evidence			
Next steps			
D – School/College organisation			
7. Leadership	i. A named member of the governing body, senior management team and the lead professional responsible for gifted and talented education have clearly directed responsibilities for motivating and driving gifted and talented provision. The head teacher actively champions gifted and talented provision	i. **Responsibility** for gifted and talented provision is **distributed**, and evaluation of its impact shared, at all levels in the school/college. Staff subscribe to policy at all levels. Governors play a significant supportive and evaluative role	i. Organisational structures, communication channels and the deployment of staff (e.g. workforce remodelling) are flexible and creative in supporting the delivery of **personalised learning**. Governors take a lead in celebrating achievements of gifted and talented pupils
Evidence			
Next steps			

	Entry	Developing	Exemplary
8. Policy	i. The gifted and talented policy is integral to the school/college's inclusion agenda and approach to personalised learning, feeds into and from the single school/college improvement plan and is consistent with other policies	i. The policy directs and reflects best practice in the school/college, is regularly reviewed and is clearly linked to other policy documentation	i. The policy includes input from the whole school/college community and is regularly refreshed in the light of innovative national and international practice
Evidence			
Next steps			
9. School/College ethos and pastoral care	i. The school/college sets high expectations, recognises achievement and celebrates the successes of all its pupils ii. The school/college identifies and addresses the particular social and emotional needs of gifted and talented pupils in consultation with pupils, parents and carers	i. The school/college fosters an environment which promotes positive behaviour for learning. Pupils are listened to and their views taken into account. ii. Strategies exist to counteract bullying and any adverse effects of social and curriculum pressures. Specific support for able underachievers and pupils from different cultures and social backgrounds is available and accessible	i. An ethos of ambition and achievement is agreed and shared by the whole school/college community. Success across a wide range of abilities is celebrated ii. The school/college places equal emphasis on high achievement and emotional well-being, underpinned by programmes of support personalised to the needs of gifted and talented pupils. There are opportunities for pupils to use their gifts to benefit other pupils and the wider community
Evidence			
Next steps			
10. Staff development	i. Staff have received professional development in meeting the needs of gifted and talented pupils	i. The induction programme for new staff addresses gifted and talented issues, both at whole school/college and specific subject/aspect level	i. There is ongoing audit of staff needs and an appropriate range of professional development in gifted and talented education. Professional development is informed by research and collaboration within and beyond the school/college

Definitions for words and phrases in bold are provided in the glossary in the Quality Standards *User Guide*, available at www2.teachernet.gov.uk/gat.

© Crown copyright 2005

Generic Elements	Entry	Developing	Exemplary
	ii. The lead professional responsible for gifted and talented education has received appropriate professional development	ii. Subject/aspect and phase leaders have received specific professional development in meeting the needs of gifted and talented pupils	ii. Priorities for the development of gifted and talented provision are included within a professional development entitlement for all staff and are monitored through performance management processes
Evidence			
Next steps			
11. Resources	i. Provision for gifted and talented pupils is supported by appropriate budgets and resources	i. Allocated resources include school/college based and nationally available resources, and these have a significant and measurable impact on the progress that pupils make and their attitudes to learning	i. Resources are used to stimulate innovative and experimental practice, which is shared throughout the school/college and which are regularly reviewed for impact and best value
Evidence			
Next steps			
12. Monitoring and evaluation	i. Subject and phase audits focus on the quality of teaching and learning for gifted and talented pupils. Whole school/college targets are set using prior attainment data	i. Performance against targets (including at pupil level) is regularly reviewed. Targets include qualitative pastoral and curriculum outcomes as well as numerical data	i. Performance against targets is rigorously evaluated against clear criteria. Qualitative and quantitative outcomes inform whole school/college self-evaluation processes
	ii. Elements of provision are planned against clear objectives within effective whole-school self-evaluation processes	ii. All elements, including non-academic aspects of gifted and talented provision are planned to clear objectives and are subjected to detailed evaluation	ii. The school/college examines and challenges its own provision to inform development of further experimental and innovative practice in collaboration with other schools/colleges
Evidence			
Next steps			

E – Strong partnerships beyond the school

13. Engaging with the community, families and beyond	i. Parents/carers are aware of the school's/college's policy on gifted and talented provision, contribute to its **identification** processes and are kept informed of developments in gifted and talented provision, including through the School Profile	i. Parents/carers are actively engaged in extending provision. Support for gifted and talented provision is integrated with other children's services (e.g. Sure Start, EAL, traveller, refugee, **LAC** Services)
	ii. The school/college shares good practice and has some collaborative provision with other schools, colleges and the wider community	ii. There is strong emphasis on collaborative and innovative working with other schools/colleges which impacts on quality of provision locally, regionally and nationally
Evidence		
Next steps		
14. Learning beyond the classroom	i. There are opportunities for pupils to learn beyond the school/college day and site (extended hours and out-of-school activities)	i. Innovative models of learning beyond the classroom are developed in collaboration with local and national schools/colleges to further enhance teaching and learning
	ii. Pupils participate in dedicated gifted and talented activities (e.g. summer schools) and their participation is recorded	ii. Coherent strategies are used to direct and develop individual expert performance via external agencies e.g. HE/FE links, on-line support, and local/regional/national programmes
	i. A coherent programme of enrichment and extension activities (through extended hours and out-of-school activities) complements teaching and learning and helps identify pupils' latent gifts and talents	
	ii. Local and national provision helps meet individual pupils' learning needs e.g. NAGTY membership, accessing outreach, local enrichment programmes	
Evidence		
Next steps		

Definitions for words and phrases in bold are provided in the glossary in the Quality Standards *User Guide*, available at www2.teachernet.gov.uk/gat.

The Eco-indicator worksheet

Production

material or process	amount (kg)	indicator	result
Total			

Use

material or process	amount	indicator	result
Total			

Disposal

material or process	amount	indicator	result
Total			

References

Barkley, R. A. (1990) *Attention Deficit Hyperactivity Disorder: a Handbook for Diagnosis and Treatment.* New York: Guilford Press.

Baylis, T. (1999) *Clock This.* London: Headline Book Publishing Ltd.

Biggs, V. (2005) *Caged in Chaos: A Dyspraxic Guide to Breaking Free.* London: Taylor & Francis.

Coren, G. (1997) *James Dyson Against the Odds.* London: Orion.

Davies L. T. and DATA (2005) *Bright Ideas Series* (www.data.org.uk).

Department for Education and Employment (1997) *Excellence in Schools.* London: DfEE.

Eyre, D. (2004) *The English Model of Gifted and Talented Education.* Paper presented at the 9th Conference of the European Council for High Ability, Pamplona, 10–13 September 2004.

Eyre, D. (2005) *Gifted and Talented in Education.* PowerPoint presentation. The National Academy for Gifted and Talented Youth (NAGTY) Conference proceedings, 27 June 2005.

Kurchinka, M. S. (1998) *Raising Your Spirited Child.* NY: Harper Perennial.

NACCE (2000) *All our Futures: Creativity, Culture and Education: National Campaign for the Arts.*

Ofsted (2003) *Handbook for Inspecting Secondary Schools.* London: Ofsted. (www.ofsted.gov.uk/publications/docs/hb2003/sechb03/hmi1360-01.html)

Ofsted (2003) *Inspection of Local Education Authorities; Ofsted/Audit Commission Inspection Guidance.* December 2003 v1a.

Sacks, O. (1995) *An Anthropologist on Mars: Seven Paradoxical Tales.* London: Picador.

Wallace, B. (2000) *Teaching the Very Able Child.* London: NACE/David Fulton Publishers.

Wallace, B., *et al.* (2004) *Thinking Skills and Problem-Solving – an Inclusive Approach.* London: NACE/David Fulton Publishers.

Webb, J. T. and Latimer, D. (1993) 'ADHD and Children Who Are Gifted', *ERIC EC Digest #E522.* (ericec.org/digests/e522).

Webb, J. T., Meckstroth, E. A. and Tolan, S. S. (1982) *Guiding the Gifted Child: a Practical Source for Parents and Teachers.* Scottsdale, AZ: Great Potential Press.

Willard-Holt, C. (1999) 'Dual Exceptionalities', *ERIC EC Digest #E574* (ericec.org/digests/e574).

Wiltshire, S. (1991) *Floating Cities.* London: Michael Joseph.

Websites

Design and Technology Association (www.data.org.uk)
Design Council (www.designcouncil.info/inclusivedesignresource)

DfES Standards Site (www.standards.dfes.gov.uk).
Dyslexia Association (www.bdadyslexia.org.uk)
Google Sets (labs.google.com/sets).
National Curriculum in Action (www.ncaction.org.uk)
One Look (www.onelook.com)
SETNET (www.setnet.org.uk/cgi-bin/wms.pl/44)
Young Engineers for Britain (www.youngeng.org)
Young Foresight (www.youngforesight.org)